IN
Bloom

GROWING, HARVESTING,
AND ARRANGING
HOMEGROWN FLOWERS
ALL YEAR ROUND

COMPANIONHOUSE
BOOKS

Clare Nolan

First published in Great Britain in 2019 by Kyle Books, an imprint of Kyle Cathie Ltd, Carmelite House, 50 Victoria Embankment, London EC4Y 0DZ, www.kylebooks.co.uk

This version published by CompanionHouse Books™, an imprint of Fox Chapel Publishers International Ltd.

ISBN 978-1-62008-328-4

CompanionHouse Books project team
Vice President–Content: Christopher Reggio
Editor: Laura Taylor
Designer: David Fisk

Kyle Books project team
Photographer and Stylist: **Clare Nolan**
Design: **Lucy Gowans**
Project Editor: **Sophie Allen**
Editorial Assistant: **Isabel Gonzalez Prendergast**
Production: **Caroline Alberti**

The Cataloging-in-Publication Data is on file with the Library of Congress.

This book has been published with the intent to provide accurate and authoritative information in regard to the subject matter within. While every precaution has been taken in the preparation of this book, the author and publisher expressly disclaim any responsibility for any errors, omissions, or adverse effects arising from the use or application of the information contained herein.

Fox Chapel Publishing
903 Square Street
Mount Joy, PA 17552

Fox Chapel Publishers International Ltd., 7 Danefield Road, Selsey (Chichester), West Sussex PO20 9DA, U.K.

www.facebook.com/companion-housebooks

Printed in China
10 9 8 7 6 5 4 3 2 1

My love affair with flowers

As a stylist in the early days of my career working on interiors for magazines, I experienced beautiful flowers in the form of stunning displays at product launches and worked with them on photoshoots, but I didn't necessarily have the budget to buy them for myself and make them part of my own world at home. When my raiding and foraging for flowers became out of hand, I had to do something, so I started growing my own – first in giant wooden planters made from scaffolding boards set out on the concrete of my London back garden, and then, when my name got to the top of the waiting list at our local allotment site, I upscaled things there by growing flowers in among my vegetables. Now that I've moved to the countryside, where I've been able to put my roots down in every sense, I've planted a dedicated cutting patch at the bottom of my cottage garden. It's sometimes a juggle – with work, two toddlers who like to remove all my plant labels, and a dog that likes to dig – but it's a dream come true.

I've been gardening ever since I saw my first red lettuce on a school trip to a market garden and wanted to grow one myself. I graduated to sunflowers, then tomatoes, and by that time I was hooked. Planting cut flowers brings that "grow-your-own" excitement to a whole new level – being able to step out of the back door and pick a single stem to go beside the bed, pull together a bouquet for a friend to take home, or cut an armload of annuals for a party is a joy. Flowers are an emotional marker through our lives, a symbolic gesture to mark our rights of passage – moments of joy, sadness, passion, and love. It's unbelievably special to honor these with your garden-gathered blooms.

Growing your own also gives you a connection to nature. Once you're hooked on flower growing (and, trust me, you will be), you'll start weather watching, you'll notice things more, you'll see things clearly. If the evening air feels nippy, you'll wonder if you need to fleece your newly planted dahlias to protect them; if you spy rain clouds on the horizon, you'll consider heading outside to pick those first precious roses before the deluge batters their petals.

OPPOSITE, LEFT: Cosmos.
OPPOSITE, RIGHT: A classic late-summer mix of roses and dahlias with lots of grasses.
OPPOSITE/BOTTOM: My potting shed, where the growing process begins with seed sowing and ends with conditioning my flowers.

Another thing I love is being able to grow flowers that I could only dream about getting my hands on otherwise – it's exciting to hunt for new, interesting varieties to try each season. For me, it's an extension of styling my home. Choosing what to grow is so personal – the plants I've selected for this book are the ones I love to fill my house with and look at. They are, on the whole, blooms that perform in the garden as well as the vase – many with knockout scent to boot. There are some plants I simply don't bother growing, as I don't like them, they aren't strong growers, or they don't fit my style. I hope you will compile your own list, adding your favorites, perhaps alongside mine from this book.

Growing your own cut flowers allows you to control not only what you plant but also how you grow and when you pick them. I'll let some flowers go to seed to harvest for their seed pods – the delicate, papery, puffed-up heads of nigella, the opaque, glass-like disks of honesty, and the dried pom-poms of scabious are all stunning and will provide you with material that feels right for the season in your arrangements. I might ruthlessly strike before a bloom is in its prime just because I like the look of the bud. Picking flowers at different stages of development to use in the same arrangement really adds a natural, garden-grown feel – you just don't get that with store-bought flowers.

Yes, it's an investment in time, but it's 100 percent worth it. There's something so special about heading into the garden after a long day with the kids or at work and coming back with a few flowers for the house. It's like having the best flower shop in the world at the bottom of your garden just waiting for you and your pruning shears.

OPPOSITE: My little garden helpers, Alexander and William, and my constant companion, Monty, our Brittany dog; roses in the window of my potting shed.

ABOVE: Roses and sweet peas in the early evening light of late summer.

LEFT: Beauty in the imperfect, rain-mottled roses.

1 Getting started

Choosing your blooms

This is your chance to dream – there'll be plenty of time to think about the practicalities later. It's time to think about which flowers make your heart sing and imagine the blooms that will be filling the vases in your home. For me, it's all about being able to grow things you can't buy in shops easily – or, if you can, they are hard to come by and expensive.

BECOME A MODERN-DAY PLANT HUNTER

Track down flowers that you love in friends' gardens, or that you see at horticultural shows. Let your heart (and nose) guide you, not a catalog – colors can be misleading in print (as can the sometimes lofty descriptions). One of my prized flowers for cutting is Rosa 'Yves piaget', a ridiculously blousy rose with a heady scent that stopped me in my tracks on a work trip to Paris once and now has pride of place in my cutting patch.

TAKE INTO ACCOUNT YOUR PERSONAL STYLE

Go for what you love rather than following trends. In the past I've grown certain flowers because I felt I should, because they were the color or flower of the moment and all over Instagram. It's simple: if you don't really love something, you won't bother picking it. Save yourself the time and energy and use the precious growing space for something you chose from the heart.

BE AWARE OF YOUR SIGNATURE COLORS

If your home is floor-to-ceiling muted heritage colors and your wardrobe a sea of neutrals, you may want to reflect that in your palette of plants. Having said that, don't let personal style and home decor limit your choice; a bucket of cottagey flowers can work as well in a modern scheme as a traditional country one. Let your heart lead you and you won't go far wrong.

BE OPEN-MINDED

The fruiting branches of red currants and raspberries, a trail of nasturtiums, or a stem of not-quite-ripe tomatoes all look just as beautiful in an arrangement as a typical cut flower does. Be brave and try something new to you, even if everyone else thinks it a little eccentric. If you grow your own fruit and veg, or can persuade someone who does to let you raid their patch, try out berries and tomatoes, and give raspberry leaves, dill, fennel, basil, angelica, and apple mint a go – they add another layer of scent.

OPPOSITE: Discovering dahlias at a flower show.
CLOCKWISE FROM TOP LEFT: 'Silver Spring' allium;
Luciano Giubbilei's stunning planting at Chelsea
Flower Show many years ago inspired me to
plant 'Buckeye Belle' peony and bronze fennel in
my cutting garden; Dahlias at a flower show; I
keep sketchbooks where I'll make notes of any
inspiring ideas I come across.

What makes a good cut flower?

The beauty of growing your own cut flowers is that you don't have the same constraints as commercial growers: there's no transportation involved that could damage delicate petals; no market forces dictating one color is in and another out. There's no supplier demanding a certain stem length or blooms that last for a minimum of ten days or the worry of something not being profitable or too labor intensive. However, there are certain traits that will make one flower more appealing than another, both in terms of its performance in the garden and as a cut flower.

IN THE VASE

STEM LENGTH The longer the stem, the more versatile it is. Avoid any varieties than are labelled "compact" or "dwarf" as they may limit how you can arrange your blooms. Some short growers are still worth it for me: muscari and lily of the valley fall into this category.

LONGEVITY Some flowers simply don't last long. Sometimes, their fleeting beauty is enough. You'll be lucky if sweet peas are still looking good after five days, while you may only get a day from some of the most highly scented garden roses once they've hit full bloom. Choosing the right variety can help extend vase life.

SHEDDING

There are flowers that leave what seems like a trail of destruction in your home: the pollen from some lilies can stain furnishings or clothing when it falls; and catkins shed and deposit a thin layer of pollen dust on surfaces. Then there's spring blossom that blooms and quickly shatters to leave a confetti-like trail through the house as you take it out to the compost bin. I still bring all of these indoors for their beauty, and the price I pay is the cleanup afterwards – only you can decide if it's worth it.

IN THE GARDEN

It's important to remember that you're not creating a "garden" in the traditional sense – you're planting to harvest the blooms and foliage. How the plants look while growing shouldn't be your primary concern (unless of course you're going to be planting for cutting within your existing garden borders), but it's useful to think about how plants perform in the garden in terms of growth. How easy are they to grow? Are they resistant to disease or pests? How quick are they to get to harvest stage? How long can you cut them for? Keep these questions at the back of your mind when flicking through the catalogs.

THINK BEYOND CLASSIC "BLOOMS"

Growing your own means a whole other world of ingredients is open to you. An arching stem of glossy rosehips, an explosion of frothy grass, or a bunch of aromatic leaves are all ingredients worthy of the vase. Think like a florist and start to see anything as fair game.

OPPOSITE: A table full of early autumnal bounty, ready for one of my one-to-one classes, includes the last of the roses, precious tuberose, and zinnias with masses of seasonal foliage and fillers.

Think in terms of ingredients

When I first started growing flowers for cutting, it was passion led; I planted what I loved without any real planning. It worked to a degree. I had lots of beautiful blooms – roses that smelled divine, glorious armloads of tulips, and fistfuls of sweet peas – but I struggled to put together bouquets and mixed arrangements as I didn't have the quantities of foliage or fillers to mix with them. I now work backwards from the displays I want to create and think in terms of the ingredients I'll need, with everything I plant playing an important role within my displays. When building a mixed arrangement, it's important to think in terms of shape – not just the flower head itself but also the overall growth habit or form of that flower, where relevant. It'll help you create a good balance of color, texture, and shape within a display.

THE ROLES THAT FLOWERS, FOLIAGE, AND FILLERS PLAY

THE HEROES

These are the stars or the showstoppers, the focal point of a mixed arrangement and the beauties that catch your eye first. They tend to be the largest, showiest flowers in the display – normally these are large, round-headed flowers such as roses, peonies, and tulips.

THE SUPPORTING ACTS

Being secondary to the stars, these flowers are still beautiful in their own right, but they compliment rather than overtake the heroes – they can contrast or harmonize with the stars. The flowers you use will depend on which hero flowers you select – they should be smaller, but still catch your eye. You can introduce more than one secondary flower. It's a good idea to mix up shapes, maybe using a spike or spire, such as on a snapdragon or larkspur, to add height, as well as a smaller, round-headed flower, such as on a small zinnia or cosmos, to help fill in any gaps.

THE FILLERS

Background flowers – the extras – along with foliage provide the bulk of an arrangement and are a chance to add texture and a little airiness. They bridge the gap between the hero flowers and supporting acts. Love-in-a-mist, lady's mantle, and white lace flower are all fillers.

THE FOLIAGE

Foliage acts as a foil to the flowers. Think in terms of layers of foliage: sturdier stems bring structure and height to a display, while fillers or soft foliage bridge the gap between flowers, pad out, and add texture. There's always room for special foliage – a trail or an arching stem that adds a little whimsy.

THE SIDEKICKS

These provide a little bit of quirk, an element that will be unique to you: a twisted stem, a trail of a flowering vine, or an unusual bloom in an unexpected color. These unexpected additions add the magic and personality to the vase arrangement.

LEFT: Ingredients laid out ready for arranging: peonies as the hero flower, plumes of masterwort to act as a secondary flower and to add height; love-in-a-mist as filler; cotoneaster tree as structural foliage, and mint as the soft foliage, with curvy stems of bishop's flower and a trail of love-in-a-puff to add a little quirk and whimsy.
BELOW: The finished display.

PLANNING FOR A GOOD HARVEST

Once you've worked out your ingredients, it's also essential to think in terms of each season to ensure you have sufficient material to pick throughout your growing year. I see it almost like a recipe; I start with my hero flowers and note when they are going to be in flower, then add the other ingredients I know will work well with them. For example, I sow a batch of hardy annuals such as bishop's flower, honeywort, and love-in-a-mist in autumn so that they will be in flower to mix with the last of the spring bulbs such as late tulips and narcissi. At the same time, I'll be able to pick granny's bonnet and some early mint.

LEFT: An autumnal color palette spotted during a visit to one of the nursery exhibits at Hampton Court Flower Show.
BELOW: A bucket of spring flowers – fritillaries, narcissi, tulips, white borage, and granny's bonnet.
OPPOSITE: Color studies for 'Hot Chocolate', 'Abraham Darby', and 'Koko Loko' roses.

Consider color, scale, texture & scent

Take the time to enjoy the process of choosing your blooms, foliage, and fillers – it's a chance to put together your version of the most perfect flower shop in the world, right in your own back garden. What makes a flower appealing is very personal: it could be a particular color you are drawn to again and again, or a beautifully intoxicating scent that beguiles you, or perhaps you fall for the strokable lush texture of velvety petals. Whatever your floral passion, indulge yourself and follow your heart.

COLOR

Color is so subjective; a shade of vivid pink may cheer one person, yet may irritate another. I'm not a huge fan of yellow in the garden or the vase, but you may love it. I'm not going to tell you which colors you shouldn't plant in your garden nor encourage you toward others because they are on-trend or of the moment. Color works on a subconscious level and is linked closely to emotion, so the best approach is to trust your instinct and go for the colors and combinations that you love.

You'll be automatically drawn to one color (or colors) over another, probably finding it easiest to decide first on your "hero" flowers (see page 14) – the ones that will become the focal point of an arrangement: such as roses, peonies, or tulips. You then need to pull together a color palette of supporting flowers (see page 14), fillers, and foliage that will work with these to form your arrangement or bouquet.

LET NATURE INSPIRE

It's helpful to look to the seasons for inspiration; each one has a personality and a color scheme of its own – an instant, perfectly formed color palette right there outside your window.

SPRING This season is full of optimism and has a freshness that other seasons can lack. The vivid acidic greens of the flush of new growth are a welcome sight after winter. Spring combinations have a lightness and a vibrancy to them and might include lime-greens, primrose-yellow, and hyacinth-blue as well as the soft blush of spring blossom.

LEFT: A moody ruby-red palette of 'Red Charm' peony, chocolate cosmos, 'Darcey Bussell' and 'Burgundy Ice' roses, and 'Sooty' sweet william mixed with copper beech leaves and 'Purple Kisses' wild carrot.

ABOVE: Harmonious pastels of 'Koko Loko' rose, larkspur, and delphinium with white perennial phlox and bishop's flower create a muted palette for this arrangement.

SUMMER This season has two faces – the rich, jewel-like colors of hot pinks, yellows, purples, and ruby-reds while the herbaceous borders reach their prime with spring greens moving to richer hues. The flip side (and my personal favorite) are the colors that have become washed out over time, fading as the season goes on. They have a romantic feel with a muted, pared-back color palette that might include the soft pinks of garden roses, elegant off-whites, and delicate peach and apricot.

AUTUMN The intense colors of autumn provide a perfect combination played out in the canopy of the trees as leaves take on tones of burnt ocher, copper, and red. Celebrate the harvest and its earthy colors of straw, pumpkin-orange, and butternut squash.

WINTER This season offers us the perfect neutral palette of an endless number of muted shades from the murky gray–blues of a winter sky and ghostly whites and silver of birch tree bark to the brooding dark greens of evergreens such as rosemary and yew. Winter is a lesson in using color sparingly – it's there if you look: the cheery yellows of mahonia, witch hazel, and winter aconite as well as the soft pink of daphne and bold red of dogwood.

WAYS TO USE COLOR IN ARRANGEMENTS

❋ Go for one color: If you want to keep things simple, stick to one color and combine lighter and darker variations. Mixing shades of a single hue will create a more muted monochromatic display. Add interest by varying scale and textures.

❋ Work in harmony: Colors that sit next to each other on the color wheel will always look harmonious in the vase. Blues and purples will feel tranquil, while red and oranges are more energetic.

❋ Use contrast: Contrasting colors that sit directly opposite each other on the color wheel will give your floral arrangement a more energetic feel. Mix red with green, or yellow with purple or blue to create a vibrant display.

A WORD ON "GREENERY"

Foliage doesn't have to be green – consider it an equal in terms of bringing color to your arrangements. There's the silvery gray of dusty miller, the deep plum of copper beech, and the warm yellows and oranges of *Heuchera* 'Caramel'. Even green foliage plants often have variations of color through the seasons, going from vibrant acidic green in spring to the changing colors of autumn as the leaves take on hues of red, orange, and copper.

LEFT: A bucket of high-contrast early-summer pickings: rich reds and pinks of 'Madame Butterfly' snapdragons and wine-colored dahlias and roses contrast with the violet larkspur and blue-green of honeywort.

SCALE

Consider the proportion of your home. If you have tall ceilings, the scale of arrangements needed will be very different to that of a small cottage, where it might take only a few small posies to make the house feel full of flowers. Think about where you want to position your blooms – there's no point growing masses of towering giants if you're looking for posies to place beside your bed and to cluster on the coffee table.

TEXTURE

The mood and feel of a flower are greatly influenced by its texture. There are blooms that are reminiscent of luxury fabrics: the deep purple, almost black petals of 'Black Jack' dahlia or *Salpiglossis sinuata* 'Black Trumpets' look like satin and silk – their deeper, darker color exaggerating the richness. Icelandic poppies have the crumpled charm of tissue paper as they unfurl, while some parrot tulips have a molded-from-plastic quality that makes you question if they are actually real. Textural blooms allow you to add another layer of interest to an arrangement and help you alter the visual weight of a display: light and airy vs. rich and solid.

ABOVE, LEFT: 'Kenora macop-B'. ABOVE, RIGHT: Foraged cherry blossom is a perfect springtime large-scale arrangement. OPPOSITE, TOP: The wax-like sculptural flower heads of 'Purple Parrot' tulips with scented lilac. OPPOSITE, BOTTOM: Artistic splodges and painterly marks on 'Rosetta' cosmos with 'Burgundy Ice' rose, 'Marble Ball', and 'Edge of Joy' and 'Lankon' lily dahlias.

SCENT

When selecting which flowers to grow, fragrance comes pretty high on my list. If you choose carefully, you should be able to add scent to pretty much every arrangement you make. We all react differently to fragrance, and it's entirely personal whether you find the generously scented *Lilium regale* or *Jasminum officinale* deliciously exotic or sickly and intoxicating. While planning your cutting garden, try to be more aware of scent – the best way to find out what you like is to take time to smell the roses. Using scented foliage is another way of bolstering the scent content of your cutting garden – the scented *Pelargonium* 'Attar of Roses' has a wonderful, rose-like fragrance.

ARTISTIC FLAIR

Splodges and splatters, freckles and spots and painterly-like strokes are some of my favorite features to look for when selecting plant varieties. They add a beauty and interest that is so rare in store-bought flowers and are always a talking point in an arrangement.

Time for a reality check

Once you've worked out the exciting part of what you want to grow – the types of flowers, foliage, and fillers and the color palette you want to work to – it's time for a bit of a reality check before you can make your dreams come to life. Let's think about the boring stuff for a second: time, money, and space. How much of each do you have to play with?

You'll need to decide how and where you intend to grow your plants. Are you planning a dedicated cutting patch to pick from? Are you aiming to add just a few rows of blooms to your vegetable garden? Or are your existing garden borders the only space you have to play with? It's possible to grow enough blooms for your house in each scenario.

ABOVE: Roses, peonies, and lupins in the perennial border in early summer.
OPPOSITE: Icelandic poppies growing alongside chard in the raised beds in my vegetable patch.

GROWING WITHIN YOUR EXISTING BEDS & BORDERS

If you already have an established garden, it's probably brimming with suitable cut-flower material already – if you can bear to cut it. You just need to change how you view your garden – cutting from it may take a bit of getting used to. If you want just a few posies for the house each week, it's perfectly feasible to have a stunning display in the garden as well as giving you plenty of material for the house by adding a few more cut flower-friendly shrubs and perennials and filling in any gaps with annuals.

GROWING ALONGSIDE YOUR VEGGIES

Flowers and vegetables make perfect bedfellows. The blooms encourage pollinators in the garden, which, in turn, ensure more vegetables and fruit for your table. When you're growing flowers alongside your veggies, you really do begin to see them as a crop and they never feel too precious to cut. Treat them as you would your veggies and grow them in rows or blocks. There's no need to worry too much about crop rotation – just try not to grow the same flowers in the same place each year. In my vegetable garden, I plant bulbs or tubers that will stay in the ground year after year (such as narcissi, grape hyacinths, and fritillaries) at the edges or end of the beds so that they won't be disturbed if I need to plant over them or to dig.

WHAT KIND OF SOIL DO YOU HAVE?

Soil is divided into five types: clay, sandy, loam, chalky, and silty. This describes their composition and gives you an indication of how free-draining or moisture-retentive it is. It's worth knowing what your soil type is as it effects how a plant will thrive and how much drainage and organic matter you'll need to add to improve your soil. To test your soil, take a look at it and feel it – search online for "soil type" and you'll see plenty of info on what to look for.

WHAT IS THE SOIL'S PH?

Soil pH is a number that describes how acidic or alkaline your soil is. You need to know whether your soil is acidic (that is, below pH7) or alkaline (that is, above pH7) because some plants, such as lilies and hydrangeas, require different pH levels. Soil testing is quick and easy to do – you can pick up a kit from your local garden center, and you'll get your result within minutes. Knowing the pH of your soil will save a lot of heartache, trust me.

ABOVE: A raised bed dedicated to cut flowers; dusty miller, pincushion flower, and love-in-a-mist are planted in rows to form blocks. Sunflowers grow alongside tomatoes and honeywort in the bed behind.

OPPOSITE: A permanent planting of roses (alongside narcissi bulbs, which are out of season in this photograph) and buxus hedging flank each side of the path to the greenhouse.

GROWING IN A DEDICATED FLOWER PATCH

It will be much more productive if you can grow your flowers and foliage in rows and blocks, because they are so much easier for planning, planting, weeding, and picking.

❋ It makes things easier to separate plants into type so that you have a permanent planting area for shrubs, perennials, and bulbs that are left in the ground and then another area for annuals – remember you are creating a productive garden not designing a garden in the normal sense. In my garden, I have a dedicated border for perennials and shrubs – it's filled with roses, peonies, phlox, pincushion flowers, a few climbing roses, and a clematis against a willow fence.

❋ I also have a dedicated "spring" border, which is planted with spring bulbs that stay in the ground from year to year: narcissi, grape hyacinths, and fritillaries. I've left areas of the bed bulb-free so that I can mingle in plantings of biennials and autumn-sown hardy annuals. I'll plant over the top of the bulbs with half-hardy annuals once the bulb foliage dies back. It's a truly hardworking patch and I'm cutting from it from mid-spring to autumn.

❋ All the annuals are planted out in a series of raised beds within the vegetable garden, either mingled in among the vegetables or by themselves – I love being able to change what I'm growing each year.

POSITIONING YOUR PATCH

❄ Most flowers like to bask in the sun, so choose the sunniest spot you have. If you have only a shady space available, your choice will be limited, but it's still possible to grow plants for cutting (see Shade-Tolerant Plants, page 174).

❄ Choose a sheltered spot – wind is not your friend as it will pummel taller stems and even the most stringent staking may fail. You can add windbreaks by putting in a willow fence or planting a hedge.

❄ Don't feel you have to relegate your patch to somewhere out of sight. Despite constant picking, my cutting garden is still one of the prettiest parts of my garden. Just be aware that if it's looking stunning, you may be more reluctant to harvest.

❄ I find raised beds are an easy way of growing flowers – a bed 4 ft (1⅛ m) wide is a comfortable size to ensure that you aren't stepping on the soil while tending or picking. You'll need a path in between beds of around 20–24 in (50–60cm) to allow access.

SHADE-TOLERANT PLANTS

While it's true that most flowers we tend to grow for cutting like to bask in full sun, there are some that tolerate a bit of shade.

Foliage and fillers: mint, lady's mantle), masterwort, honesty.

Hero flowers: hellebores, hydrangeas, snowball bush.

For secondary flowers: Solomon's seal, bleeding heart, Japanese anemones.

Bulbs: snowdrops lily of the valley.

TIME ON THE PLOT/PATCH

You could make growing your own flowers a full-time pursuit – it will swallow as much time as you have to give it. However, you need to be realistic about the time you can commit. Start small, if necessary, and reign in your dreams just a little, for a season or two, until you've found your feet. I only manage to keep vaguely on top of my garden alongside everything else in my life by splitting the time I do have into small chunks. I'm still amazed by what can be achieved in a series of 10- or 15-minute slots.

TIME-SAVING TIPS

❊ Do your weeding little and often so you catch weeds early. Use a hoe to decapitate weed seedlings, and they'll shrivel to nothing within hours on a hot day. Growing in rows makes weeding so much quicker. I personally don't use weed-barrier plastic, but professional growers do as it keeps weeds down to a minimum.

❊ Don't underestimate how long it takes to harvest your flowers. Planting in rows will help cut down the time it occupies. I find that color coordinating the beds also helps, as bouquets come together much more quickly.

❊ Go for some of the "plant-and-forget-about-them" plants; flowering shrubs such as lilac or viburnum won't create much work, but after a couple of years in the ground will give you masses of flowers to cut. A late-flowering clematis, such as *C.* 'princess Kate' in pruning group 3, just needs cutting down to the ground each spring and in return you'll be able to pick flowering trails for months.

❊ Installing a drip-irrigation system will save you hours of watering a week in a hot summer (it's also a very efficient way of watering, as there's very little lost to evaporation).

❊ Buy your plants as potted plants instead of growing them from seed yourself. Or simply sow seed directly in the garden in spring; although you'll have a shorter growing season, possibly with more casualties to slugs and snails, you won't have to bother with potting and transplanting into the garden.

❊ Start small – a wigwam of sweet peas, a row of narcissi followed by dahlias, and a row of hardy annuals such as love-in-a-mist, honeywort, and bishop's flower for filler and foliage will give you something to pick in spring, summer, and right up to the first frosts Then add more plants as and when time allows.

MONEY

It's perfectly possible to grow a flower patch from a few packets of seed with very little expense, but costs soon start to mount up if you want to cultivate lots of varieties and add perennials and shrubs. To help keep costs down, grow as much as you can from seed, take cuttings, and divide your plants to build up stock. Source any bought material for your cutting garden as bare-root plants as it's more cost-effective than "garden-ready" potted plants. I also swap seeds and seedlings with friends as I rarely ever use a whole packet of seed.

ABOVE: A section of one of the beds in the cutting garden in late summer – nasturtiums alongside mixed grasses.
OPPOSITE: Roses, lupins, and peonies in the perennial bed.

Sourcing your plants

A great deal of the success of your cutting garden comes from the planning and preparation you put in, not only in terms of your site and soil, your choice and combination of flowers and foliage, and the planting plans, but also in terms of sourcing your plants. A well-considered cutting garden allows you to order what you want at the right time of the year so you avoid those knee-jerk, impulsive (and expensive) buys. You'll end up getting much better value for your money, and your plants will get off to a flying start.

OPPOSITE; TOP LEFT: Dahlia cuttings bought from a specialist grower online – they will be flowering within a few months. OPPOSITE, TOP RIGHT: A trolley of nursery-grown shrubs and perennials to expand my cutting garden includes ninebark, coral bells, and Japanese anemones. OPPOSITE, BOTTOM: Cuttings from my friend Marion – my favorite sort of present.

GROWING FROM SEED

I start most of my annuals and biennials from seed. Many are easy to grow, and there's a million and one different varieties to choose from, which allows you to try new things each year. It also helps keep the cost down – seeds are cheap. You'll often see annuals on sale potted up as "garden-ready" plants later in the season for the same price as a few packets of seed that provide hundreds of plants. It makes sense to grow your own. It's totally possible, even if you don't have a greenhouse and you're a complete beginner.

Most of my seed sowing happens in early spring – the busy period for gardeners, with smaller batches occurring in midsummer and autumn. There's lots more detail on this later (see pages 44–59). If I need a large number of a perennial plants, I'll grow those from seed, too – it's exactly the same principle as for annuals and biennials, although some need a little more care and attention.

BUYING SEEDLINGS

These can be very useful if you've mistimed your sowings. I'll often put off sowing biennials in midsummer when there's so much else going on, a week goes by, then two, then a month – before I know it, I've missed the opportunity entirely. An online order of baby-sized biennial plants for transplanting out in autumn can save the day.

ORDERING BARE-ROOT PLANTS

Before the invention of the plastic pot, many more plants used to be bought this way. The plants are delivered in their dormant period in winter, without soil. You may take one look at these unpromising bare sticks and naked roots and think nothing will ever come of them, but they will come back to life in spring – they're just having a bit of downtime. Bare-root plants are a great way to source unusual varieties of many flowering plants, including roses, peonies, and dahlias, and it's cost-effective, too. The window for bare-root plants is normally from winter to very early spring, and each plant will need to be put in soil straight way, weather permitting.

BUYING BULBS

The best way to source your bulbs, corms, and tubers is to buy them when dormant or dry, as you pay a premium for them potted up and already in growth. Spring-flowering bulbs get planted from the beginning to the end of autumn; summer- and autumn-flowering types go in during spring. You want to get your order in a couple of months before planting time to ensure you get the varieties you're after. I prefer to buy bulbs online from reputable suppliers as I know they will be stored in the correct conditions, instead of in a heated shop floor of a garden center. Online supplies also offer so much more choice in terms of varieties.

POTTED PLANTS

This is the most expensive way to source your cut flower material, but someone else has done the sowing, nurturing, and tending for you. I'll sometimes buy perennials in pots if they're a type that I can't give the time and attention they need to grow from seed, or if I don't require masses and I want to save myself some hassle. It's also a good idea to buy shrubs as medium or large potted plants so you aren't waiting forever to harvest from them – hydrangeas, viburnums, and ninebark all fall into this category for me. Potted plants are available year-round.

BUILDING UP STOCK

If you have the time, propagating your own plants is a fantastic way of building up stock for your garden, especially for the more expensive ones. You can do this by taking stem or root cuttings, dividing plants, or growing from saved seed – it's so rewarding and, of course, it's free. I love it when a friend gives me a cutting and there's a story behind a plant in my garden. I sometimes buy plants specifically to use for propagating. You'll be able to take multiple cuttings from one plant and still have the mother plant afterwards. There's no great skill involved, but a little patience is required. (See How to Take Cuttings of Scented Geraniums, page 202.)

GET TO KNOW YOUR PLANTS

ANNUALS & BIENNIALS

An annual completes its life cycle by germinating, growing, flowering, setting seed, and dying within the space of a year. Split into hardy and half-hardy, the former can tolerate frost, whereas half-hardy annuals can be planted out in your garden once there is little risk of frost.

Biennials complete their life cycle within two years: germinating and putting on foliage growth in the first year and then flowering, setting seed, and dying in the second. They are generally hardy plants that tolerate frost as they have to overwinter in the garden in their first year. They are started from seed in the midsummer of their first year and then flower in late spring of their second. Examples include foxgloves, sweet williams, and honesty.

BULBS

A term often used to cover corms, rhizomes, and tubers as well as true bulbs. All are self-contained – storing enough food and nourishment within themselves to survive until the next season and flower. Generally, they are planted in spring or autumn. Some can be left in the ground where they will naturalize, spread, and come up each year, while others are lifted and dried after flowering and replanted for the following season, and the process repeated. There are also some that are treated as one-hit wonders – pulled up and discarded after they flower. Tulips, daffodils, and ornamental onions are all bulbs.

PERENNIALS

These are non-woody plants that live for many years, getting bigger and better each year. They have stems that remain above the ground during winter. Some are "short-lived'"and may last for only a few years. Many perennials are relatively easy to grow from seed and may even flower in their first year. In general, their cutting season is between early summer and the end of autumn.

HERBACEOUS PERENNIALS

These differ in that all stems die back in late autumn or early winter. The roots remain under the soil in winter and then the stems reshoot in spring.

SHRUBS

Shrubs are evergreen or deciduous plants that have a woody framework that persists above the ground through winter. They differ from trees in that they are multistemmed, rather than single stemmed like a tree. Once they are established, they provide an abundance of cutting material. Hydrangeas, viburnums, and roses are all shrubs.

CLIMBERS

True climbers have a natural climbing habit – some even self-cling. They generally take up very little ground space and are an interesting addition to the cutting garden. Clematis, honeysuckle, and some roses are all examples of climbers.

OPPOSITE, TOP LEFT: A bare-root
dahlia looks unpromising, but it will
be pumping out blooms within a few
months.
OPPOSITE, TOP RIGHT: Gladioli corms.
ABOVE: Seedlings have been hardened
off in the cold frames and are now
ready to be planted out in the garden.
ABOVE, RIGHT: Snapdragons and
nasturtiums in one of the raised beds
with salvia and pincushion flower in
the bed behind.

The tools

There are all sorts of fancy tools for seemingly every single gardening task man has ever thought of, but the following are the ones I use on a very regular basis. For essential floristry tools, see page 230.

Decent pruning shears: These are worth spending a bit of money on. I prefer the bypass types as they work like scissors and give a clean cut. I have two sizes: one for cutting stems and one that can get through small branches. Keep shears clean and sharp.

Flower snips: For deadheading, pinching out, and cutting herbs and some thinner-stemmed flowers.

Wheelbarrow: If you're going to be tending anything bigger than a couple of beds, it's worth buying a wheelbarrow to save yourself the hassle of carrying everything yourself. You can get away with a plastic bin with handles if you're working something small.

Digging spade: Choose one that suits your body in terms of its weight and length – I've got one with an extra-long handle, which suits me as I'm tall. My spade has footrests so I can stand on it in my boots.

Digging fork: Again, I've got one with a longer handle as that's what suits me.

Hoe: For weeding seedlings on the surface of the soil, using a hoe for 5–10 minutes every now and then saves so much time later.

Rake: This is invaluable for prepping the ground for sowing and planting out.

Hand trowel and hand fork: I use copper-alloy hand tools – they are not cheap, but look stunning and perform well.

Pen knife: A sharp, general-purpose knife can be used for everything from cutting twine to taking cuttings.

Garden knife: I'd been using a retired kitchen bread knife in the garden for years before I discovered hori-hori knives existed. Mine has one serrated and one smooth edge – it's my new favorite tool for dividing plants, cutting roots, or weeding.

Plastic bin with handles: These are really useful for collecting weeds, mixing compost, moving or soaking plants, or filling with water and using to drench planting holes.

Watering cans: For watering small areas and applying feeds you need a watering can. A gentle spray head is essential for watering small plants.

Hose: If you intend to have only a few small beds, you can make do with a watering can. Otherwise, spend a bit of money on a hose, as cheap ones will soon kink and it's really annoying to have to walk to the other end of the hose to straighten it out the whole time. I'm upgrading to a drip-irrigation system for next season as it will save so much time and is a much more efficient way of watering.

Garden sprayer: These are useful to apply homemade feeds and tonics to small plants. I use a mini version in the greenhouse to mist seedlings and cuttings.

Gardening gloves: I wear these at every opportunity to save my hands and my nail polish.

Planting ideas

The choice of plants available for the cutting garden is endless. Without knowing your personal preferences for color, type of flower, etc., along with your soil type and the amount of space, sun, and shade you may have to play with, any "planting plan" in the traditional sense that I might put together may not be of much use to you at all. Instead, my aim is to inspire you with planting ideas, and give you confidence to make the choice about varieties and individual plants yourself, to create the perfect flower garden for you.

ADDING CUT FLOWERS TO YOUR EXISTING GARDEN

❋ Look at your existing garden through the eyes of a florist, not a gardener and give yourself permission to cut anything you like the look of (that may take some getting used to). Set aside any preconceptions about what you think a flower display should be – if you like the look of something, cut a few stems and try it – you only have yourself to please.

❋ Keep your plants healthy and productive by making sure your cuts are clean (tools should be sharp) and cut back to a set of leaves or buds. Try to keep things as even as you can – no picking from just one side of a shrub.

❋ If you're short on space, try and choose plants that are as productive as possible for the space they use (you may decide that foxgloves and peonies don't make your list for that reason). Put the vertical space to good use: there's always room for another climber – their vertical growth means they take up very little room.

❋ Make use of any gaps in beds and borders, either filling them with annuals or clusters of bulbs that you can leave to naturalize. Choose a good mix of cut and come-again annuals that will keep pumping out flowers, fillers, and foliage, leaving some to be enjoyed in the garden as well as picked – deadhead regularly those you have left for garden display to keep the flowers coming.

❋ If you think creatively you can plant flowers to cut where it will go unnoticed – narcissi bulbs can be left to naturalize under fruit trees or in grass, shorter narcissi or muscari can sit along the edges of borders.

❋ The secret to making the space you do have most efficient is to start plants off in pots elsewhere so that they are up and growing before the patch you're planting them into has even become available – giving you a head start. It also means that your garden is looking better for longer.

❋ For me a cutting garden would be incomplete without tulips and dahlias – they work well in pots if that is the only spot available to you. They make the perfect planting partners to share the same space – with dahlias replacing the dahlias once the tulips have finished. Plant tulips in blocks or dense clusters, really close together (like eggs in an egg carton) so that you'll have plenty to pick as well as leave to flower in the garden if you want. Once they have bloomed, pull up the bulbs and replace with dahlias. Dahlias need about 5 in^2 (30cm^2) of space per plant.

SPRING

TULIPS IN POTS

Tulips planted in late autumn will flower in mid to late spring. Pull up the bulbs as you harvest the flowers, discard the bulbs, and refresh the soil.

HARDY ANNUAL FLOWERS, FILLERS, AND FOLIAGE

Autumn-sown hardy annuals – directly sown in any gaps in your border or grown elsewhere and planted as seedlings.

HARDY OR HALF-HARDY ANNUAL FLOWERS, FILLERS, AND FOLIAGE

Autumn-sown hardy annuals – directly sown in any gaps in your border or grown elsewhere and planted as seedlings.

SUMMER

DAHLIAS

Replant the pots with dahlia tubers after the last frosts are over. To get a head start on the season, you could start the bare-root dahlia tubers off a month earlier in pots and keep somewhere frost-free undercover.

HARDY ANNUAL FLOWERS, FILLERS, AND FOLIAGE

Once the first batch of annuals starts becoming less productive, pull them up and replace with another sowing of HA or HHAs (sown direct or as seedlings). Go for long-season cropping flowers like zinnia, cosmos, or rudbeckia to give you flowers right through to autumn. Plant a row of gladioli corms in among the annuals at one end.

HARDY OR HALF-HARDY ANNUAL FILLERS, AND FOLIAGE

Once the first batch of annuals starts becoming less productive, pull them up and replace with another sowing of HA or HHAs (sown direct or as seedlings). Go for long-season cropping flowers like zinnia, cosmos, or rudbeckia to give you flowers right through to early autumn.

AUTUMN

DAHLIAS

The dahlias will go on flowering until the first frosts, then cut back the plants and pull up the tubers to store over winter somewhere frost free to use again next year (see page 124).

HARDY FLOWERS, FILLERS AND FOLIAGE

Once the second batch of annuals is slowing down and the gladioli foliage has changed color, pull up the corms and store over winter, then replant the space in early autumn with another batch of hardy annuals to start the cycle all over again.

BIENNIALS

Plant out summer-sown biennials like sweet william, foxglove, and sweet rocket to flower the following year. You can buy them as seedlings if you haven't sown any.

ONES TO SQUEEZE IN

CLIMBING ROSE

Choose a repeat flowering rose – the vertical growth can be trained close to a wall to take up less space. It will give you blooms from late spring to autumn.

SWEET PEAS

Autumn sown sweet peas can be planted out as plugs in the spring.
12 plants trained up a wigwam will give you flowers every other day for two months once they're get into their stride.

PERENNIAL BULBS

Narcissi, muscari, allium and fritillaria–plant them in clusters where you have suitable free ground – some varieties will happily naturalise in grass.

THE SMALL CUTTING PATCH

❋ A bed measuring 47 in (120cm) deep x 94 in (240cm) wide will provide you with blooms from spring to autumn if succession planted. I've chosen 47 in (120cm) as the depth of the bed so that you can easily reach across without standing on the soil. Also, the plant spacing I use most regularly for annuals divides easily into 47 in (120cm). Just make the bed longer if you have more room. If possible run the bed from east to west and plant the rows from north to south so that you aren't shading shorter plants with the taller ones.

❋ I've drawn this cutting patch as one bed, but you could separate out these "ingredients" and put them in various parts of your existing garden or divide them up and grow them alongside your veggies – they could even be grown in large pots.

❋ In a small plot like this one, it doesn't make sense to grow trees or shrubs – you'll get better return on your space by planting hardworking annuals and bulbs.

❋ To get the most flowers from your bed, you need to plant annuals closely together in blocks and rows – ignore what the seed packet says and work to the spacings on page 39.

❋ Tag-team flowers so that the same growing space is used all the way through the cutting season – replacing one spent row or block of plants with a batch of new ones. Tulips treated as annuals and pulled up after flowering can be replaced with HAs or HHAs. Once biennials have gone over, they can be replaced with HHAs.

❋ If you have space, grow seedlings in pots and rainwater gutters elsewhere so that you can get a head start and replace spent plants with jumbo seedlings that are closer to flowering.

❋ In your permanent planting areas, choose plants that make the perfect bedfellows, sharing the same soil and following on from one another. If your winters aren't too extreme, dahlias should overwinter okay with a thick mulch and work well planted over narcissi bulbs. Plant the narcissi bulbs deep during the autumn and then plant the dahlia tubers over the top (in autumn if you can get hold of them or in late spring if not).

❋ When choosing which annuals to grow think about your mix of foliage, fillers, and flowers so you get the balance right. You roughly want a 50/50 split of flowers vs. foliage and fillers. Consider their planting heights when planting out so that short plants won't be shaded by taller ones.

❋ Sweet peas will flower for about two months well; be brutal and once productivity decreases, pull them out and follow on with HA flowers, fillers, and foliage – either direct sown or as seedlings grown elsewhere. You could always follow on with a HHA climber that you've been growing in pots elsewhere – like Cobea.

GROWING ELSEWHERE

The key to ensuring a small patch is as productive as possible is to start seedlings and plants off elsewhere in your garden. That way, instead of sowing seed directly you can plant seedlings to cut down the harvest time between one crop and another.

GUTTERS OF SEEDLINGS

Direct sow annual seed into rainwater gutters and grow them in another part of your garden. Use them to fill in any gaps created when you pull up any spent annual plants or bulbs.

SEEDLINGS IN POTS

Grow on half-hardy seedlings such as the climbers cup and saucer or black-eyed Susan in small pots so that you have good-sized plants that will take over from the last sweet peas and give you flowers right up until the first frosts.

START DAHLIAS OFF IN POTS

Get ahead on the season by potting up dahlia tubers undercover – so you have decent sized plants when they are ready to plant out after there's little risk of frost.

SPRING

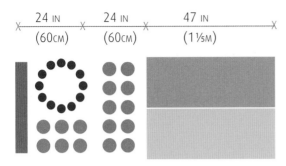

SWEETPEAS – a wigwam of 12 sweet pea plants

PERENNIAL BULBS - Muscari or multiheaded narcissi along the edges of the bed

HARDY ANNUALS - Autumn-sown hardy annual flowers, foliage, and filers – sown direct or planted as seedlings.

NARCISSI – bulbs planted in the autumn – will flower, then die back at the end of spring

TULIPS – planted in autumn – treat as an annual and pull up the bulb as you pick for extra stem length

SUMMER

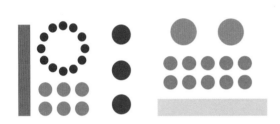

SWEETPEAS – will flower for about two months well; once the productivity decreases, cut them down and follow with direct sown or seedlings of HA flowers, fillers, and foliage.

HA/HHA FLOWERS, FILLERS, AND FOLIAGE – once the first batch slows down, pull up and replace with a second batch.

DAHLIA – watch out for new growth to appear just as the narcissi foliage is beginning to die back and protect from slugs.

SUMMER BULBS – add a row or two of summer bulbs like gladioli among the annuals.

AUTUMN

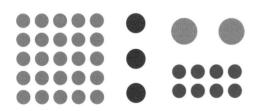

DAHLIA – the dahlias will keep flowering right through to the first frosts, then cut them back to the ground and mulch for the winter.

BIENNIALS – follow on from the annuals with biennial plants – sown in mid-summer and grown on to jumbo seedlings. The summer bulbs will need pulling up and storing over winter.

HARDY ANNUAL FLOWERS, FILLERS, AND FOLIAGE – once the first batch slows down, pull up and replace with hardy annuals for early flowering next spring.

KEY

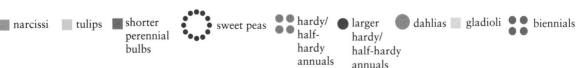

narcissi | tulips | shorter perennial bulbs | sweet peas | hardy/half-hardy annuals | larger hardy/half-hardy annuals | dahlias | gladioli | biennials

A LARGE CUTTING GARDEN

❁ The same principles apply to a large cutting garden as they do for a small patch, it's just a question of scaling things up and adding perennials, shrubs, and trees into the mix. When you have more room to play with, it makes sense to separate the plants into growing type – planting perennial bulbs in one bed (or series of beds), your herbaceous perennials in another, annuals in another, and so on. It makes everything much easier to tend and harvest, as well as plan for.

❁ As with the beginner's garden on the previous page, I would suggest making the beds 47 in (120cm) deep – running east to west so that rows can be planted north to south to form blocks of plants. Make the beds as wide as you'd like, but bear in mind that if you make them too long, you won't be bothered to walk around and you'll end up trampling and compacting your soil.

❁ Allow yourself a path of around 20-24 in (50-60cm) in between, with a wider path of about 39 in (1m) down the center for wheelbarrow access.

❁ It makes sense at this point to think about a greenhouse or a series of cold frames if you have the space and the budget – at the very least consider a heated propagator and grow light to make propagating easier and quicker (not to mention more enjoyable).

❁ A plant for cutting is only useful to you if it's productive; once production slows down, be brutal and pull it up and replace it with something else. When planning, think in terms of space and time – how much space will a plant take up and how long will it be in the ground for? I grow seedlings in 2 ¾ in (7cm) pots or rainwater gutters elsewhere in the garden, so I have a supply of seedlings waiting in the wings to plant once one batch has gone over.

THE DREAM ELEMENTS

❁ In an ideal world, with limitless money, time, and energy, we might have all of these elements in our cutting gardens. Until then, pick and mix and go as small or large as your space allows.

❁ Trees and large shrubs – if you have the luxury of space, consider planting trees for blossom and flowering branches and shrubs to give you long stems of through the year. It's an investment of both time and money as it takes a while before they'll be ready to harvest, but once they're established they'll give the garden year-round structure and height as well as keeping you in cutting material. In an exposed garden, plant trees and shrubs to create a windbreak to protect your plants. And plant on a north-facing boundary so they do not cast shadow on the rest of the garden.

❁ Perennials – it's a delight to be able to raid a perennial bed and not have to worry about how it will look afterwards. Keeping your perennials in one bed and growing them in rows or blocks helps you think of them as a crop, not a garden display. Plant larger shrubs in threes and smaller in fives or sevens to give plenty to harvest from. Check the heights and spreads of the plants – you can position them a little closer together in a cutting garden.

❁ Sweet peas in rows – growing your sweet peas in rows makes tending and picking much easier. Plant them out with about 8 in (20cm) between plants in two rows per 47 in (120cm) wide bed.

❁ A dahlia bed – double up in your growing space by either planting tulips or narcissi in the same bed. If you lift your dahlias each to overwinter them inside, use the space for tulips (pulling the bulb up as you pick). If you keep your dahlias in the ground – plant narcissi bulbs (plant the naricissi first and the tubers on top). Plant the dahlias about 24 in (60cm) apart.

❁ A rose bed – repeat-flowering roses will bloom heavily first in early summer with another flush later in the year – some varieties will gently re-bloom through the summer. As a general guide, plant the roses about 24 in-39 in (60cm -100cm) apart – one or two rows per bed. I plant narcissi bulbs and hardy annuals like nigella in the space surrounding them.

❁ Mint bed – mint can be a bit of a brute in the garden as spreads quite aggressively via its roots. It's best to contain the plant to one large pot or container – or give it a bed all of its own. It will need lifting and dividing every four years or so.

❁ Allow yourself paths for tending and harvesting.

PLANT SPACING

When growing plants for cutting it's possible to grow the plants closer together than you would normally in your main garden. I think in terms of creating blocks of plants – just as I do for vegetable growing to maximise production. For most of the annuals I grow, in a bed that's 47 in (120cm) deep, I'll plant out rows of 5 plants (at a spacing of roughly 9 in x 9 in [24cm x 24cm]), building up blocks of varying sizes depending on the number of plants I want. I find a block of two or three rows is normally enough for my needs as I prefer to grow small quantities of lots of different varieties. It's a method I've used successfully for years and after learning more from Washington, USA-based flower grower extraordinaire, Erin Benzakein of Floret Flower Farm and her high-intensity production techniques, I've added a couple of her spacing regimes to mine – tweaking them slightly for a 47 in (120cm) border.

6x6 in (15x15cm) (8 plants in a row per 47 in [120cm] bed, 47x47 in [1⅕x 1⅕m] = 64 plants)
Perfect for annuals with a more upright growth like single sunflowers or larkspur.

9x9 in (24x24cm) (5 plants in a row per 47 in [120cm] bed, 47x47 in [1⅕x 1⅕m] =25 plants)
The spacing I use the most for annuals; cerinthe, snapdragons, Icelandic poppies all do well at this spacing.

12x12 in (30x30cm): (4 plants in a row per 47 in [120cm] bed, 47x47 in [1⅕x 1⅕m] =16 plants)
For plants that bulk up a little more like foxgloves or branch more like Queen Anne's lace. A good spacing for a mint bed.

16x16 in (40x40cm): (3 plants in a row per 47 in [120cm] bed, 47x47 in [1⅕x 1⅕m] =9 plants)
For plants with large side branches, like the branching sunflowers or amaranthus.

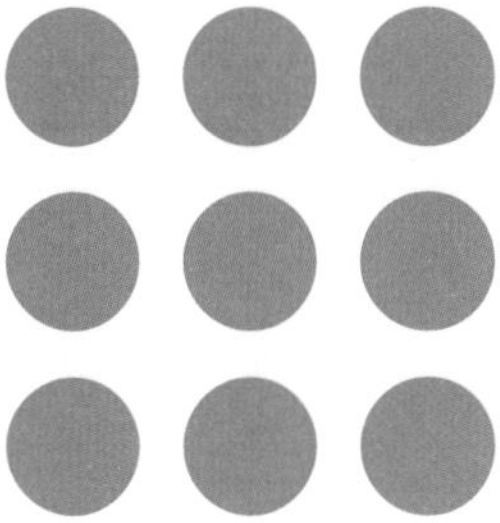

24x24 in (60x60cm): (2 plants in a row per 47 in [120cm] bed, 47x47 in [1⅕x 1⅕m] = 4 plants)
A general spacing suggestion for roses, but it does depend on the growth habit and variety. It's also a good spacing for dahlias.

INGREDIENTS' CALENDAR

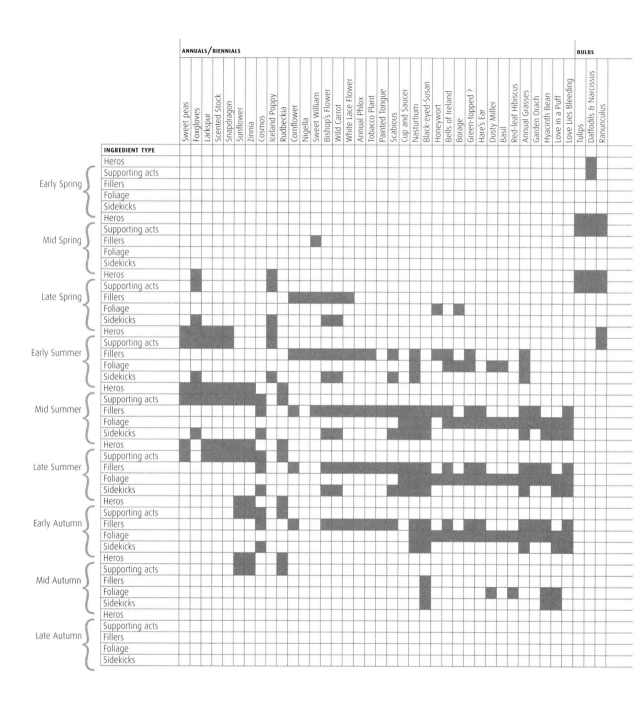

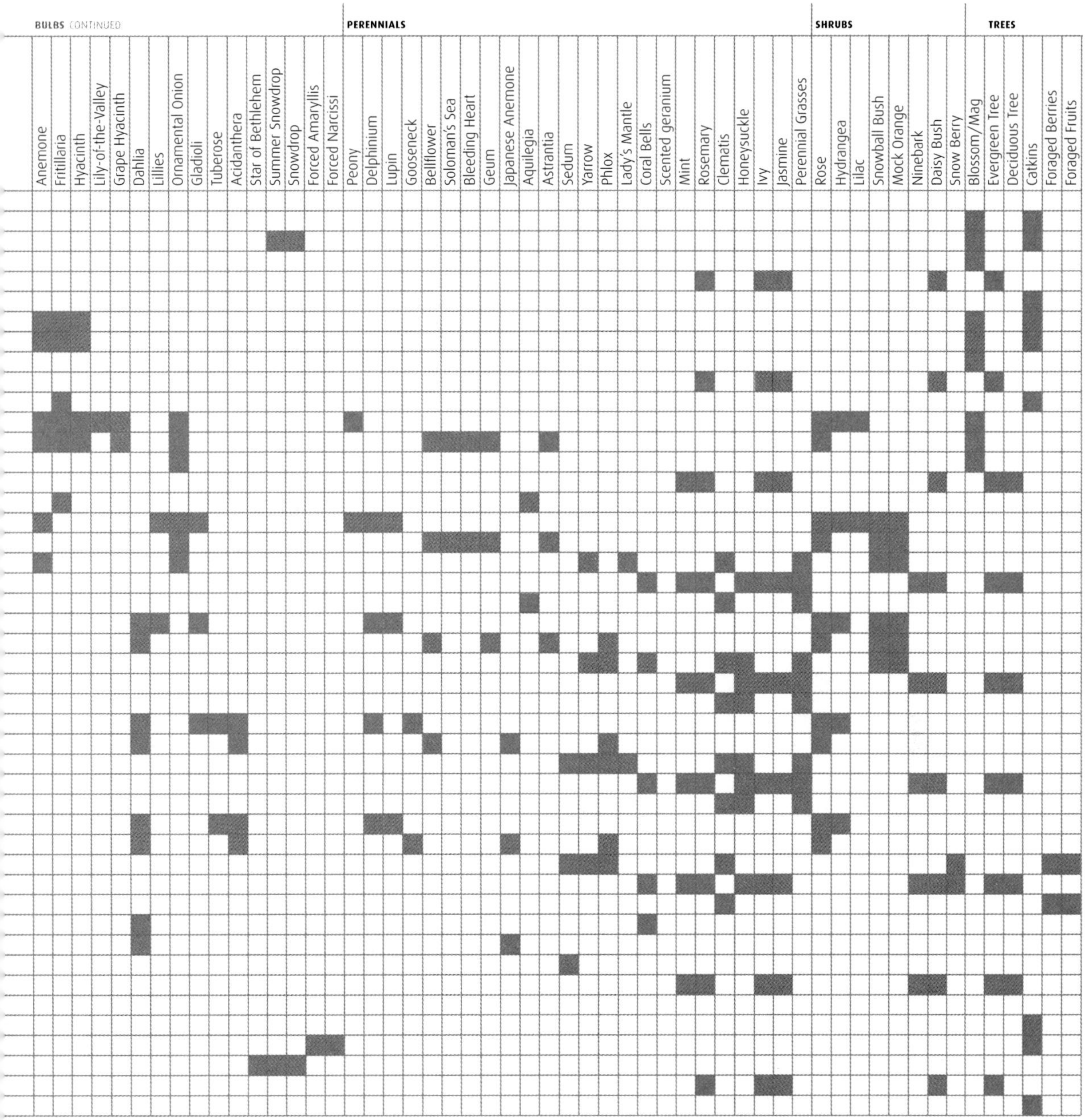
BULBS CONTINUED
Anemone
Fritillaria
Hyacinth
Lily-of-the-Valley
Grape Hyacinth
Dahlia
Lillies
Ornamental Onion
Gladioli
Tuberose
Acidanthera
Star of Bethlehem
Summer Snowdrop
Snowdrop
Forced Amaryllis
Forced Narcissi
PERENNIALS
Peony
Delphinium
Lupin
Gooseneck
Bellflower
Soloman's Sea
Bleeding Heart
Geum
Japanese Anemone
Aquilegia
Astrantia
Sedum
Yarrow
Phlox
Lady's Mantle
Coral Bells
Scented geranium
Mint
Rosemary
Clematis
Honeysuckle
Ivy
Jasmine
Perennial Grasses
SHRUBS
Rose
Hydrangea
Lilac
Snowball Bush
Mock Orange
Ninebark
Daisy Bush
Snow Berry
TREES
Blossom/Mag
Evergreen Tree
Deciduous Tree
Catkins
Foraged Berries
Foraged Fruits

The flower grower's year

SPRING

EARLY SPRING

✳ Sow half-hardy annuals like amaranthus, cosmos, and zinnia undercover about 6-8 weeks before the risk of frost in your area has passed.
✳ Direct sow hardy annuals like cerinthe, nigella, and cornflower once the ground warms up.
✳ Start off anemone corms and ranunuclus claws by soaking and pre-sprouting (page 63), grow on undercover.
✳ Start off dahlia tubers in pots undercover.
✳ Plant out autumn sown sweet peas and sow another batch of seed for follow-on flowers.
✳ Order late summer/autumn flowering bulbs and biennial and perennial seed (to sow in mid-summer).

MID SPRING

✳ Continue to sow hardy annuals direct for a succession of flowers.
✳ Prick out seedlings grown undercover and pot, continue to grow on indoors, potting again if needed (watch for little white roots trying to escape out of the holes at the bottom of the pot).
✳ Plant summer/autumn flowering bulbs. Plant gladioli bulbs in small batches every couple of weeks for the next two months for an extended flowering season.
✳ Begin to harden off plants started off indoors, begin with the hardy annuals first, then the half-hardy annuals.
✳ Plant out hardy annuals once they are hardened off properly. These can go out about a month or so before the risk of frost has passed, but watch out for any potential hard frosts and use fleece to protect if necessary.

LATE SPRING

✳ Continue to harden off plants and seedlings started indoors – putting them outside on warm days and the plant out once risk of frost has passed.
✳ Once hardened off, plant out all seedlings and plants started indoors – keep an eye on the weather and protect with fleece if a rogue late frost is forecast.
✳ Position supports where needed before the plants put on too much growth.
✳ Keep an eye on the moisture levels and begin watering if it's a dry spring.

SUMMER

EARLY SUMMER

✳ Continue to sow batches of annuals for follow-on flowers – pulling up plants once they become less productive and replacing them with new ones. Think of anything sown before mid-summer as this season's crop – anything sown after will be for the next season the following year.
✳ Make homemade comfrey tea (page 55) and start feeding plants every two weeks a seaweed feed and then the tea once it's ready. Give heavy feeders a bit extra; I give my roses a specialist rose feed that is high in potassium and apply a good-quality tomato feed to my dahlias.

MID-SUMMER

✳ Sow perennials and biennials like foxgloves, sweet william, and honesty for flowers next year.

LATE SUMMER

✳ Order spring/early summer flowering bulbs like alliums, daffodils, lilies, anemones, rannunculus, and tulips to ensure you get the varieties you want.

AUTUMN

EARLY AUTUMN

❋ Plant out mid-summer sown biennials like foxgloves, sweet william, or honesty.
❋ Sow hardy annuals like cerinthe, nigella, and cornflower for early flowering next year either direct or undercover to overwinter indoors.
❋ Plant spring/early summer flowering bulbs like daffodils, alliums, and lilies (but not tulips yet).
❋ Start off anemone corms and ranunuclus claws by soaking and pre-sprouting (page 63), then planting out or overwintering in a greenhouse.
❋ Collect seed from spend blooms, clean and either sow immediately or store for the following season.

MID AUTUMN

❋ Sow sweet peas
❋ Plant out potted perennial plants and shrubs.
❋ Divide perennials to increase stock.
❋ Dig up and store gladioli bulbs, and dahlia tubers if your garden is very cold or the soil is wet.
❋ Clear beds and prepare for the following season – apply mulch of well-rotted compost and manure.

LATE AUTUMN

❋ Plant tulip bulbs.
❋ Pot up bulbs like paperwhites and amaryllis for forcing over winter.

WINTER

EARLY WINTER

❋ Plant bare-root trees and shrubs.

MID-WINTER

❋ Check on dahlia tubers and gladioli corms stored overwinter – watch for any signs of mold and water sparingly if they are starting to shrivel.
❋ Order annual seeds

LATE WINTER

❋ Sow slow-growing annuals like larkspur and cup and saucer.
❋ Prepare the ground for sweet peas if weather permits – digging in plenty of well-rotted manure or compost and fix the supports in place.
❋ Sow a second batch of hardy annuals undercover.

2 Annuals & biennials

The powerhouse
of your cutting garden

Annuals and biennials are most likely to provide you with the main bulk of
material in your cutting garden, at least to begin with until your perennials
and shrubs hit their stride. They are quick to grow, cheap to buy, and prolific,
and there really is one for every purpose and taste. Annuals complete their life
cycle within a year, while biennials take two – forming foliage in their first year
before flowering in their second. I grow all mine from seed, which opens the
choice of cut flowers a thousandfold – I get to grow unusual varieties that just
aren't available to buy as plants at nurseries or garden centers.

GROWING FROM SEED

A packet of seed is full of possibilities – it still amazes
me that a tiny seed contains all that potential. There's
a sense of unequalled satisfaction to be gained as your
first seedlings of the season emerge and make their way
in the world. Sowing from seed also allows you a sense
of extravagance without much cost at all. If you want to
plant swathes of cosmos, a packet of seed will give you all
the plants you'll need at a fraction of the price of buying
the equivalent in potted plants from the garden centre.

HARDY VS. HALF-HARDY

Most biennials tend to be hardy as they need to make
it through their first winter before flowering, but not all
annuals are. Half-hardy annuals can't take any frost and
need to be started off and grown on under glass and
planted out only when there is little chance of frost –
otherwise they'll turn to mush. Hardy annuals can handle
frosts and even take a slight freeze. They can be sown
direct in spring, or in autumn for earlier flowering and
bigger plants the following spring.

RIGHT: Seedlings ready to be pricked out
and potted.
OPPOSITE: *D.* x *purpurea* 'Sutton's Apricot'

SOWING DIRECT

You can direct sow hardy annuals in spring and/or autumn and some half-hardy annuals in early summer. It's super easy – it's all about preparation.

Dig and rake the soil over, breaking up any clods of earth and getting rid of any large stones – you want the soil to resemble the fine topping of a fruit crumble. Tread the soil down by walking over it once or twice in your boots, to get rid of any air pockets. Then you're ready to sow. Follow the instructions on the seed packet but bear in mind the spacing distances recommended on page 56 when you come to thin out the seedlings.

SOWING UNDER COVER

Sowing indoors allows you to grow your own half-hardy annuals from seed and get a jump start on the season with hardy annuals.

❋ While it's perfectly possible to grow seeds inside on a bright windowsill without any special kit, you will get much better results if you invest in a heated mat or propagator and a grow light. It was a game changer for me.

❋ Most of my seeds are sown thinly into square 2 ¾ in (7cm) pots as I don't need masses of each variety and it saves on space in my propagator, but any container that holds soil and allows water to drain can be used. I also use traditional seed trays when I need more of something, and I sow sweet peas and sunflowers into root-trainers, which help to develop their larger root systems. This year, I began making my own soil blocks – where the soil acts as both the growing material and the container – it worked really well and in time I will switch over to these entirely.

❋ I always use a good-quality commercial seed soil that has been specially formulated for propagating – it's a good consistency for small seeds. For larger seeds such as sweet peas and sunflowers, I use a multipurpose potting soil.

❋ The newly sown seeds go into my heated propagator with a grow light overhead and they stay there until they have emerged and the seedlings formed a pair of true leaves (these differ in shape and color to the first leaves). Then I prick them out carefully with a pencil and pot them on individually into bigger pots, usually a 2 ¾ in (7cm) pot, and move them to my heated bench in the greenhouse where they'll stay until they are big enough to be planted out (after hardening off).

ABOVE: 2 ¾ in (7cm) pots are an efficient way for me to maximize the space in my heated propagator so I can start a large number of different varieties.
OPPOSITE: Direct sowing hardy annuals in the spring to replace the early tulips I've already harvested.

GETTING YOUR TIMING RIGHT

❋ It's tempting to start sowing seed as soon as there's a whiff of spring in the air, but don't. Seed direct sown too early will often rot or get off to a bad start and in all likelihood will probably be overtaken by later-sown plants anyway. Be patient, wait for the soil to warm up first – emerging weed seedlings are a good indicator that the time is right.

❋ The best way to figure out when to sow seed under cover is to work backwards from your last frost date. If you have no idea when this is, either ask at your local garden center or search online. There are plenty of websites that allow you to input your nearest town and give you the info you need.

❋ Most seeds sown under cover should be started off just 4–6 weeks before the last frost – most plants will be ready to make the shift to the big outdoors at this point. Sow too early and you risk the plants being ready before the ground is warm enough – resulting in leggy and, most likely, pot-bound plants.

❋ It helps to know the "days-to-bloom" for each variety – normally shown on the seed packet. Seeds with slow germination rates, or that take a while to get going, such as larkspur, stocks, and snapdragons need to be started off a little earlier than most annuals – which are started off 4–6 weeks before the last frosts. Some biennials, such as hollyhocks, sweet williams, and foxgloves, will flower in their first year if you sow them early enough.

❋ There are some exceptions: hardy annuals can take a bit of cold so they can be sown earlier and planted out as young plants up to a month or so before the last frosts, as long as there's no chance of the ground freezing. For me, this is about four weeks before the last frost in my area.

OPPOSITE: Potting biennial foxgloves and hollyhock seedlings into 2¾ in (7cm) biodegradable mesh bags.

PLANTING

Generally, a plant is ready to go out in the garden when it has about three or four sets of "true" leaves – these differ in shape to the first pair of leaves the seed produces when it emerges. However, I tend to wait until plants are a little bit bigger than this, because tiny seedlings in my garden can't survive the trampling, ferocious nose-nudging and digging-up sessions from my dog, as well as attacks from a thriving local slug and snail population.

HARDENING OFF INDOOR SEEDLINGS

After the mollycoddling you've given your seedlings indoors, you need to prepare them by hardening them off to lessen the shock of the move to outdoors. Over the course of 2–3 weeks, begin increasing their exposure to outside, to toughen them up. My "springtime shuffle" consists of moving seedlings from the heated bench to the cold greenhouse, then the cold frame before planting them in their final positions outdoors. You can achieve the same hardening-off process by putting seedlings somewhere sheltered by a wall or hedge, covered with a couple of layers of horticultural fleece, during the daytime for the first week of exposure and bringing them in at night. For the second week, take off one of the layers of fleece during the day, leaving two on at night. Then in the third week, remove the fleece during the day altogether, taking it off at night toward the end of the week before planting out the following week. It's all a little bit of a palaver, but without it the plants go into shock and won't do very well at all.

ABOVE: Foxglove seedlings coming up in soil blocks made using a "Micro 20" block maker. These biodegradable mesh bags are a good alternative to plastic pots.
OPPOSITE: Larkspur seedlings beginning their hardening off process.

TOP: Homemade comfrey feed being applied to 'Attar of Roses' scented geranium – it should be the color of weak tea.
ABOVE: 'Madame Butterfly' snapdragons supported with pea netting.
LEFT: Sweet peas climbing up a hazel wigwam and pea sticks.

LOOKING AFTER YOUR ANNUALS & BIENNIALS

FEEDING

I feed my annuals and biennials every two weeks with a seaweed foliar feed or a homemade comfrey feed (see below), to keep them producing. It's really easy to make your own.

A HOMEMADE FEED FOR YOUR PLANTS

I recommend you find space to plant some comfrey (*Symphytum*). It makes a brilliant high-potassium feed for your plants, which will encourage blooms. Comfrey can be quite a thug and difficult to get rid of – it grows back from the tiniest bit of root if you leave any in the ground – so make sure you really want it where you plant it. *Symphytum × uplandicum* 'Bocking 14' is a non-seeding strain so it won't self-seed around your garden.

MAKING COMFREY TEA

❋ Chop up the leaves and put them in a bucket or container – you'll want to use something with a lid as this "tea" becomes quite pungent once it starts rotting.

❋ Cover the leaves in water – using a brick or a stone to weigh them down.

❋ After 4–6 weeks the leaves will have broken down and the liquid will be brown in color. Drain off the liquid through a sieve into a container

❋ Dilute – 1 part comfrey tea to 30 parts water – to feed your plants every two weeks. It's not an exact science – the darker the liquid is, the more you'll need to dilute – you're aiming for a weak tea color.

❋ Top up with fresh leaves and more water for another batch of feed.

WATERING

Regular watering is up there with good soil in terms of plant health and maintaining flower production. Water at the base of the plant rather than from the top. In an ideal world, install a drip-irrigation system or a leaky hose. If you can't do that, use a hose with a long arm so you can get the water to where it needs to go.

SUPPORT

Most annuals and biennials require support to help keep stems upright. It's not about keeping the stems poker straight. It doesn't take much for stems to start to flop about: in a heavy shower of rain, the stems will be pushed toward the ground and then develop an elbow-like, 90-degree bend as they try to grow toward the sun again.

For annuals, I find the best support is wide-gauge netting stretched horizontally over the plants at the start of the season; the plants grow up and through the netting, eventually covering most of it. This works best when you're growing in a straight border in rows. In my mixed borders, I'll use twiggy pea sticks or a series of canes with a zigzag of string between them to create a spider's web of support.

GETTING THE MOST FROM YOUR PATCH

❋ Successive sowing: Sowing seed in small batches at regular intervals helps to extend your harvest and prevent a glut – there's no point in having everything ready to pick within four weeks and then nothing for months.

❋ Autumn sowing of hardy annuals: As a gardener, I rarely feel ahead of the game. There's always something I should have done and a to-do list as long as my arm, because the season seems to fly by. One thing that helps me feel like I'm getting ahead is sowing a batch of hardy annuals such as love-in-a-mist, bishop's flower, honeywort, and cornflowers in autumn. You'll get bigger plants than spring-sown ones and earlier blooms – up to four weeks earlier, extending your flowering season even more.

❋ Sow in guttering: I sow seeds in recycled guttering that I've cut down to the same width as my rows. It means I've always got something waiting in the wings that's up and running to replace something that is winding down.

FINAL SPACING

When you are growing plants for cut flowers you can afford to plant much more densely than traditional wisdom allows, so ignore the advice on the back of the seed packet. It's a trick I learnt from flower farmer extraordinaire Erin Benzakein of Floret Flower Farm, and since following her advice on planting spaces I've grown so many more flowers in the same plot.

Here's my planting spaces regime in my 47 in (1 ⅕m) beds:

6 x 6 in (15 × 15cm) – for tall, single-stemmed flowers such as sunflowers and larkspur.

9 x 9 in (24 × 24 cm) – for most annuals: love-in-a-mist, snapdragons, and Icelandic poppies.

12 x 12 in (30 × 30cm) – for bulkier plants such as cosmos, bishop's flower, foxgloves, and amaranthus.

16 x 16 in (40× 40cm) – for large plants with a branching habit such as branching sunflowers.

OPPOSITE, LEFT: Harvesting zinnias – cutting toward the end of the stem to a pair of sideshoots - I'll come back for the those two flowers another day.

OPPOSITE, RIGHT: Honeywort seedlings planted at 9 in (24cm) spacings.

LEFT: Cornflower seedlings coming up in guttering – I'll slide these into a spare row in one of my raised beds.

PINCHING OUT

Pinching out the growing tips encourages annuals to bush out and produce more flowering stems. It's best to do this when the plants are young – when they are 8–12 in (20–30cm) high. Either snap off the growing tip between finger and thumb or else use a pair of flower snips. You want to be taking off about 4 in (10cm), back to just above a set of leaves. Plants that produce only one flower per plant, such as single-stemmed sunflowers or stocks, don't need to be pinched out.

MAKING THE CUT

When I first started growing my own flowers, I was a little scared when it came to harvesting and made the mistake of cutting too high up the plant – thinking I might do harm if I cut too low. Actually, the opposite is true for most annuals. With annuals that have a central stem, such as zinnias, the first cut early in the season needs to be near the base of the plant – much closer to the ground than you might think, just above three to four sideshoots. This is to encourage a more branching habit and stronger stems. After this first cut, the rest are made toward the end of each stem being cut.

FLOWERING HABITS

THE CUT-AND-COME-AGAINS

Harvesting flowers has the same effect as deadheading, but instead you are cutting them just before their moment of glory. If you keep picking, annuals like cosmos and zinnias will go on producing new flowers until they become so exhausted they stop flowering at the end of summer. When you are cutting, make sure that you leave some sideshoots intact – these will provide the next lot of flowers.

THE ONE-HIT WONDERS

Plants that produce only one flower per plant on a single stem, such as non-branching sunflowers and stocks, need to be planted in succession (around every two weeks) to extend their flowering period.

THE MULTIPLE BLOOMERS

These have a similar habit to the cut-and-come-agains, but they become exhausted sooner and will stop flowering well after a while. Larkspur and honeywort fall into this category. I do two or three sowings of these multiple bloomers to extend my harvest through the season.

Collecting seed

In terms of horticultural highlights, the only thing more rewarding than growing your own flowers is to grow them from seed that you have collected yourself. It's pure magic. Sadly, it's a skill that we're losing connection with as we rely more and more heavily on imported seeds, but it's actually very easy to get started. Be warned though, once you start you'll be hooked and you'll want to try more; before you know it, you'll be pilfering borders for ripe seedheads and squirrelling away the seeds in your pockets like I do.

ABOVE, LEFT TO RIGHT: *Cerinthe major* 'Purpurascens', *Scabiosa atropurpurea* 'Beaujolais Bonnets', Nigella *damascena* 'Double White', *Nicotiana langsdorffii*, cosmos, *Borago officinalis* 'Alba', *Campanula persicifolia* var. alba, *salvia viridis* 'pink', and *Cardiospermum halicacabum*.

These are my top tips for seed collection and are a great place to start, as not all seed can be saved.

✽ Look for varieties that are described as "open-pollinated" or "heirloom" rather than "hybrid" (often labelled as F1) as they are more likely to come true to type – that is, have the same characteristics as the parent plant.

✽ Choose strong, healthy plants. Tie a ribbon around a stem of a plant you particularly like when it is at its peak so that you can identify it more easily when you come to collect seed.

✽ Be on seed watch. You want to catch seeds just as they ripen but before they disperse. Generally, this means when the seedheads have turned brown, dried out, and can be easily split by hand to access the seed.

✽ Ideally, it should be a warm, sunny day when you come to collect. Snip the seed pods/heads off and put them straight into a small brown paper bag. If there's a risk of the seed going everywhere, you might want to put the bag over the whole flower head before you snip. Label it and leave to dry somewhere warm, but out of direct light – for example, on a windowsill or in an airing cupboard – for about a week.

✽ Once the seeds are completely dry (the pods should crumble in your hands), it's time to clean them, separating the seeds from the chaff. All of the flower seeds above are pretty easy to separate by hand – you just need to pick through them carefully.

✽ Transfer the seeds to small envelopes, label, and store in an airtight container. If you have any spare silica-gel sachets around the house, add a couple of those too, to help absorb any moisture. Seeds are best kept somewhere dark and dry, at around 41°F (5°C) – a refrigerator is perfect.

Sweet peas (*Lathyrus odoratus*)

Heavenly scent, romantic frilliness, and prolific flowering coupled with the fact that they are pretty much foolproof and come in almost every color under the sun (bar yellow) make sweet peas one of the most popular cut flowers to grow. I love the sense of abundance and generosity they allow – I'm picking fistfuls of them every other day from late spring to summer, once they get into their stride.

The romantic gardener in me always wants to grow heirloom varieties, but I find the best ones for cutting are the later bred 'Spencer Mixed' and Modern Grandiflora and Semi-Grandiflora varieties rather than the older Grandiflora ones, which, although they bear that exquisite, famous sweet pea perfume, have fewer ruffled flowers on shorter stems. If you choose Modern Grandiflora varieties carefully, you can have the best of both worlds: amazing fragrance and long stems with plenty of frills. There is an almost overwhelming choice of varieties available. To narrow this down and make arranging easier, I think in terms of a color palette: a family of colors such as brights, vintage pastels, sultry moody darks or blues that will sit well together. I'll always have at least one white or cream in the mix and a couple of the "flaked" or "striped" varieties with spectacular markings. Many seed suppliers have started to do this for you and put together a collection of different varieties in one packet, but if you are growing in large numbers you can mix and match your own as I do.

MY FAVORITES

WHITES & CREAMS
'High Scent' (also sold as 'April in Paris') – white with purple feathering. Height 71 in (180cm).
'Aphrodite' – a long-stemmed pure white. Height 71 in (180cm).
'Juliet' – cream with a hint of soft pinky-apricot blush. Height 71 in (180cm).

REDS & ORANGES
'Valerie Harrod' – a bright orange-pink that's the color of watermelon. Height 71 in (180cm).
'Restormel' – a vivid coral-red. Height 79 in (200cm).

PINKS
'Anniversary' – white with pale pink coloring. Height 71 in (180cm).
'Prince Edward of York' – pink bicolored with a mix of deep and pale pink. Height 71 in (180cm).
'Judith Wilkinson' – an intense shade of cerise. Height 71 in (180cm).

BLUES & PURPLES
'Almost Black' –the deepest purple and, as the name suggests, sometimes nearly black. Height 71 in (180cm).
'Blue Velvet' – a rich deep blue-purple. Height 71 in (180cm).
'Abutt Blue' – pale blue edging on a pale ground. Height 59 in (150cm).

INTERESTING FLAKING OR STRIPES
'Nimbus' – white with streaks of inky-blue/black. Height 71 in (180cm).
'Wiltshire Ripple' –white with blackcurrant/chocolate flaked petals. Height 98 in (250cm).
'Earl Grey' – an unusual bicolored flaked variety that fades to blue/gray. Height 71 in (180cm).

OPPOSITE, FROM TOP TO BOTTOM: 'Lilac Ripple', 'Almost Black', 'Blue Velvet',' Wiltshire Ripple', 'Abutt Blue', 'High Scent' (two bunches) 'Juliet', and 'Aphrodite'

IN THE GARDEN

PREPPING THE SEED

Traditional wisdom is that you prepare the sweet pea seed before planting. There are a number of ways you can do this: for example, nicking the seed with a sharp knife; or soaking the seed. I've tried them all and now I don't bother – I just sow sweet peas straight from the packet, as I've found germination rates are pretty high anyway. However, it is worthwhile preparing the seed if you have problems with mice as they love feasting on sweet pea seeds and can annihilate a whole batch in one sitting. The seeds will germinate quicker, and once the seeds have sprouted and are up and running they are less appealing to the mouse.

I find the best prepping treatment is "pre-sprouting'": soak the seeds overnight then lay them on damp kitchen paper and leave somewhere warm. Check each day that the paper is still damp and mist with a sprayer if needed. Once the seeds have sprouted (it should take around five days), pot them up. It's also worth giving this a go if you've ever had problems growing sweet peas from seed before.

A GOOD ROOT RUN

Sweet pea seedlings create lots of roots, even when small, so give them a good root run. I sow mine in root-trainers, and leave them in there until I plant them out. As they spend a long time in the same soil, I use multipurpose rather than the specialist seed soil. If I'm delayed in planting them out, I'll give the young plants a feed to keep them in tip-top condition while they wait.

AUTUMN & SPRING SOWING

It's worth doing two sowings to extend your season. I do one batch in my unheated greenhouse in late autumn for early flowers and the other batch in spring – the latter can be sown direct or in pots. As the season goes on, the length of the flower stems decreases, and the plants become less productive.

PINCHING OUT

Once the plants are about 6 in (15cm) tall, pinch out the growing tip of each between your finger and thumb, just above a leaf joint, to encourage bushier plants with more flowers.

PREPPING THE SOIL

The only real work in growing sweet peas is preparing the ground properly. It pays to dig well and incorporate lots

ABOVE: Sweet pea seedlings.
OPPOSITE: Sweet peas growing in a mixed border alongside roses.

of well-rotted manure, well-rotted compost, and a few handfuls of bonemeal before planting out.

SUPPORT

Sweet peas can grow to around 79 in (2m) so will need sturdy support. Either grow them in rows with pea netting or let them scramble up wigwams made from bamboo or hazel, with pea sticks (I use prunings from the garden) to give extra support between the uprights. Weave string between any spots that are gappy. Put your support in place before your plants. They can be grown in pots, too; select a container as big as you can – the plants need the food.

PLANTING OUT

About a month before the last frosts, begin to acclimatize autumn-sown plants for three weeks or so before planting them in their final positions. I space mine about 8 cm (20cm) apart. Sweet peas take a little while to settle in and find their feet, but be patient. They'll suddenly romp away and you'll need to keep tying them into their supports, to help them upwards. I position the plants in their color families. It makes arranging so much easier – I can then bunch as I pick.

FEEDING

To get the best sweet pea blooms feed every three or four days. Avoid a high-nitrogen feed as this will give you lots of lush foliage and fewer flowers. Opt instead for a good tomato or seaweed feed.

THE TENDRIL ISSUE

Tendrils can sometimes grab onto the stems above and create a bend that makes it quite difficult to arrange the flowers (such bends are also why you keep tying in the stems to help direct them upright). The question is, do you remove them? When I had my allotment, I grew sweet peas in rows by the cordon method and painstakingly removed all the tendrils. I was rewarded with masses of straight, long-stemmed flowers, but it was a laborious task. I now don't bother at all.

KEEP PICKING

Sweet peas are quite quick to set seed if left unpicked and once that happens they'll stop producing flowers altogether. Keeping on top of picking can become a bit of a chore, so much so that I've now reduced the number of sweet peas I grow. Even with friends coming to help themselves, I used to struggle to keep on top, sometimes. I've found the best way to tackle harvesting is to go over all the plants every other day, taking all the flowers. Ideally, you want to be picking sweet peas when the top two flowers are still to open.

IN THE VASE

Sweet peas last about four or fivedays in the vase, not long admittedly, but with another flush ready to pick in a couple of days this never really bothers me. I hardly ever "arrange" my sweet peas as such – I bunch as I pick and tie with string and then plonk them in a vase on their own – the sheer abundance of their number and intensity of fragrance feels extravagant and indulgent enough. Sweet peas do look good when intermingled with other flowers, especially the flaked or bicolored ones to add a bit of extra interest. Don't overlook the curly tendrils and leaves – it's rather special to be able to add a trail or two tumbling out of an arrangement.

ABOVE: 'Wiltshire Ripple' and 'Aphrodite' mixed with gooseneck and rose.

OPPOSITE, LEFT: : A mix of sweetpeas – the bright orange is 'Watermelon'.

OPPOSITE, RIGHT: I'll often bunch as a pick – using string to tie each bunch.

Foxgloves (*Digitalis*)

This cottage-garden classic, with its tall spires of tubular blooms from late spring to midsummer so beloved by bees, has to be one of my all-time favorites. It's my perfect "pick-and-pop-in-a-vase" kind of flower; no arranging required – you just sit back and take the credit for its whimsical beauty. It brings a wildness and softness to an arrangement and a wonderful sense of movement. There's no scent, but I'm willing to overlook that.

Foxgloves are mostly biennial or short-lived perennials sown from mid- to late summer to flower the following year. Some varieties are grown as annuals, flowering in their first year after an early sowing under cover, while others are genuinely perennial and will keep returning to your garden year after year. They all make fabulous cut flowers.

MY FAVORITES

D. purpurea Camelot Series – F1 hybrids in a mix of colors including cream, soft pink, white, and lilac. With an early sowing under cover, they will flower in their first year. Height 39–59 in (100–150cm).

D. purpurea Dalmatian Series – a more compact form with a branching habit so you'll get sideshoots producing smaller secondary flowers. They flower in their first year when sown early. Height 39–47 in (100–120cm).

D. parviflora Polkadot Series – perennial foxgloves with a long flowering season. There's a lovely, gentle, white spotting to their petals that gives them a painterly feel. Height 24–39 in (60–100cm).

D. purpurea 'Sutton's Apricot' – biennial or short-lived perennial with soft pink-apricot blooms. Height 59 in (150cm).

D x mertonensis – stunning semi-evergreen perennial with beautiful, dusky pink flowers. Height 35 in (90cm).

D. purpurea subsp. *heywoodii* 'Silver Fox' – short-lived perennial with pure white flowers and strokable, downy, silvery green leaves. Shorter than most, but a beauty. Height 24 in (60cm).

TOP: *D.* x *mertonensis*.
ABOVE: *D.* x *purpurea* subsp. heywoodii 'Silver Fox'
OPPOSITE: *D.* x *purpurea* 'Sutton's Apricot', *D.* x *purpurea* subsp. heywoodii 'Silver Fox'

IN THE GARDEN

❀ Foxgloves can tolerate full sun but prefer a little bit of shade; they are at their happiest in the dappled sunlight on the edges of a woodland.

❀ For best value for money, I grow from seed. The seeds are minute so I use a damp toothpick to pick up a couple of seeds at a time and push them onto the soil surface. They need light to germinate, so don't cover them. Some people sow direct after flowering or allow the plants to self-sow, but I prefer to sow in trays so I know what I'm getting.

❀ Midsummer is the best time to do this for biennial and perennial foxgloves. I start them off outside in the cold frame and plant out into the garden about six weeks before the first frosts. If the young plants are not big enough at that point, I'll overwinter them in the greenhouse and plant them out in spring.

❀ First-year flowering annual foxgloves are best started off under cover in late winter or very early spring. I use a propagator to speed up germination and then move seedlings to the greenhouse.

IN THE VASE

❀ Ideally, pick when only a few of the bottom flowers are open. The flowers will drop from the stem quickly once they have been pollinated.

❀ Foxgloves reflower from sideshoots after the first cut, to give a smaller more delicate bloom that's very useful for hand ties or bouquets.

❀ Expect a vase life of about a week.

ABOVE, RIGHT: D. *purpurea* – the wild form of foxglove.
RIGHT: D. *purpurea* 'Camelot Lavender'.
OPPOSITE: A mix of D. *purpurea* 'Dalmation Crème' (pale yellow), *D.p.* 'Dalmation Pink' and *D.p.* 'Sutton's Apricot'.

Larkspur (*Consolida*)

Perennial delphiniums, I will admit, were my nemesis until I started growing
them in the free-draining soil of my raised beds. They would vanish from my
perennial border from one season to the next – victims of ground slugs and a
few particularly damp winters. Meanwhile, larkspur became my savior – an
easy-to-grow annual cousin of the perennial spires that had eluded me for so
long. I've come to prefer their smaller spikes over their beefier relatives.

MY FAVORITES

D. consolida 'Smokey Eyes' and 'Misty Lavender' –
exquisite varieties; both have a knocked-back, slightly
sludgy coloring that gives them a vintage feel. Height
47 in (120cm).

ajacis Giant Imperial Series 'White King' – a type that is
sturdy and free-branching – a beautiful pure white. Height
47 in (120cm)

regalais Cloud Series – bushy plants that are totally
different from the usual larkspur types; tiny flower
heads float at the ends of wispy stems to create a froth
that's reminiscent of gypsophila. 'Snowcloud' has white
flowers. Height 30 in (75cm).

IN THE GARDEN

❋ Larkspur can be a bit hit and miss when growing from
seed. Popping the seed packet in the refrigerator for a
couple of weeks before sowing helps with germination.
Either sow directly outdoors in autumn or under cover in
spring. Larkspur can be slow to germinate – sometimes
taking up to two months, so I tend to start mine early in
late winter and then plant out after the last frosts.

❋ These plants like free-draining soil in a sunny spot – I
grow mine in raised beds in rows where it's also easy to
weed and harvest.

❋ Larkspur is ready to cut when one-third of the flowers
are open. Expect the flowers to last 7–10 days in a vase.

ABOVE: *C. ajacis* 'White King'
growing in a bed with tomatoes in
the vegetable garden.
OPPOSITE LEFT AND RIGHT: *C. ajacis*
'White King' and 'Snow Cloud'
harvested with roses and potted
summer hyacinth bulbs (*Galtonia
candicans*) – another good cut
flower.

Stocks (*Matthiola incana*)

Fragrance is one of the major joys of gardening; getting a whiff of something wonderful as you're weeding or digging brings pleasure to the chore. Stocks are one of the cutting garden's hard-hitters with a knockout scent that stops you at 20 paces. It's a familiar scent that most people recognize straight away – a mix of spicy-sweet with a heavy-garden-hand of clove. Alongside their amazing fragrance, as archetypal cottage flowers, stocks have vintage good looks and they are pretty easy to grow, too.

IN THE GARDEN

❊ Stocks have two different growing habits: the "column" types are traditionally grown as cut flowers and produce a single flower head per plant, and the "branching" types, which also produce flowering sideshoots and need pinching out to encourage bushy growth and more flowers. Don't make the same rookie mistake I did and pinch out the column types, thus throwing all my potential flowers for that season on the compost heap – that was a hard lesson.

❊ Start seed 8–10 weeks before the last frost for harvesting in early spring. I sow stocks early in the year under cover for an early spring harvest.

MY FAVORITES

Vintage Antique Mix – a great mix of apricots, white, purples and pinks. Height 16 in (40cm).

Traditional Field Grown Column Stock Apricot – a pretty soft peach and 'Appleblossom' – a delicate pale pink. Height 30 in (75cm).

Katz Formula Mix – long, strong stems in a stunning mix of colors from brights to moodys, in pinks, purples, apricots, yellows, and pure white. Height 24–32 in (60–80cm).

Ten Week Mixed – usually take – you've guessed it – around ten weeks from germination to flowering; it's a super quick crop. A mix of purples, lilacs, pinks, and whites with that classic, clove-like perfume. Height 12–16 in (30–40cm).

IN THE VASE

❊ Pick when about one-third of the blossoms have opened on the stem.

❊ With such intense fragrance, one stem in a bunch of other flowers will provide plenty of scent, but I love arranging them en masse and the sense of extravagance this brings.

❊ Be sure to take off all the leaves below the waterline – stocks are super quick to make the flower water smell foul and any leaves left will just speed this up.

❊ If you keep changing the water regularly – at least every other day – stocks should keep smelling sweet and last up to ten days in a vase.

A WORD ON DOUBLE VS. SINGLE

Stocks produce single or double flowers based on their genetics. The singles are pretty, but are a world away from the supercharged doubles in both looks and scent. With modern varieties, you've roughly got a 50:50 chance of getting either, but how do you know which is which? About two weeks after sowing, when the seedlings have emerged completely, take the seed tray and put it somewhere that's below 50°F (10°C) for a week. I put mine in my unheated greenhouse, but you could also pop them in the refrigerator for three or four days (just water them well and protect them with a clear plastic bag so they don't dry out). After their period in the cold, you should be able to see a few subtle differences between the seedlings. Doubles appear a slightly lighter shade of green than the singles, and are sometimes a little taller, with more oval-shaped leaves. Once you've identified the singles just chop them down with a pair of scissors and grow the doubles as normal.

OPPOSITE: Vintage Antique Mix

Snapdragons (*Antirrhinum majus*)

Snapdragons are the kind of flower that might pass you by, dismissed as merely another bedding plant in varieties that barely graze your ankles. However, if you look beyond the trays sold at garden centers to the seed catalogs you'll discover a whole other beauty entirely. Snapdragons are also immensely productive – a real cut-and-come-again flower.

MY FAVORITES

'Madame Butterfly' (mixed) – azalea-type, frilly doubles in deep reds, bronze, ivory, pink, and yellow. I am sometimes glad of a mix as it opens me up to colors that I might perhaps never have chosen to grow as a single color myself. Height 35 in (90cm).

'Chantilly Mix' – an "open-faced," single-flowered form with ruffled petals that are almost butterfly-like. There's a wide range of colors, but for me the prettiest are the soft pastel shades. Height 55 in (140cm)

IN THE GARDEN

Although technically short-lived perennials, snapdragons are best grown as annuals. I sow mine under cover about eight weeks before the last frosts and plant them out when they are still quite small (and have only three sets of true leaves) as they can take a few light frosts. Nip out the growing tips when plants reach 6–8 in (15–20cm) high, to increase the number of flowers. Some growers don't pinch out, preferring to harvest taller larger blooms a little earlier. The plants need supporting – horizontal netting is best.

IN THE VASE

❋ When it comes to harvesting, cut low – almost to the base of the plant – to encourage long side branches. It might feel a little counterintuitive to be cutting so hard, but you will be rewarded with better blooms. Keep picking snapdragons and they'll keep producing flowers.

❋ Condition the flowers in a tall vase – they are geotropic and will bend toward the light if they are left leaning in a short bucket.

❋ Expect a vase life of 7-10 days.

LEFT: 'Madame Butterfly' (red).
OPPOSITE: 'Madame Butterfly' (bronze).

Sunflowers (*Helianthus annuus*)

The classic golden-yellow variety is one of the few flowers I make an exception for and break my "no-yellows" rule. It's pure joy and takes me back to my time spent in the south of France when I was 19 and the first time I experienced the jaw-dropping sight of fields of sunflowers stretching for miles. Alongside the classic sunshine yellows, there are soft vanilla and lemon varieties – as close to white as you'll get, intense rusts and coppers, bronzes and burnt oranges right through to the brooding burgundies. Choose between the single-stemmed varieties that will give you just one cut, which you can plant close together, and the branching types that produce multiple flowers on sideshoots coming off the central stem. You'll need more space to grow the latter, but the upside is more flowers and slimmer stems, which are much easier to incorporate into arrangements.

MY FAVORITES

'Ms Mars' – leaves and stems are tinged with dark red-purple; petals are a red-purple that turns a pretty pink. A branching type. Height 24 in (60cm).

'Procut Red' – dark chocolate centers with ruby petals with faded tips. Especially bred for commercial cut flower production. Single stem. Height 59 in (150cm).

'Superted' – taller version of frilly, yellow, fully double. 'Teddy Bear' with flowers 4 in (9cm) across. Numerous buds form all along the stem with the lead bloom being the biggest. Height 59 in (150cm).

'Valentine' – branching, primrose-yellow variety with almost black centers. My new favorite. Height 59 in (150cm).

'Velvet Queen' – deep velvety copper-red. Branching type. Height 59 in (150cm).

ABOVE: 'Superted'.
OPPOSITE, TOP: Just picked 'Valentine' with autumn grasses and a bucket of zinnias.
OPPOSITE, RIGHT: 'Procut Red', 'Valentine' and 'Sonja' in full bloom with the heads of 'Procut Red' stripped of their petals.
OPPOSITE, BOTTOM LEFT: 'Jade'.

'Sonja' – cute, petite, branching type with classic yellow sunflower looks. Height 39 in (100cm).

'Jade' – beautiful, nearly white, branching type with greenish white centers. Height 47 in (120cm).

IN THE GARDEN

Sunflowers are easy flowers to grow from seed. I start mine off in pots inside, in an attempt to evade slug attacks, but they can be sown direct once the frosts are over. There are two easy ways to extend your harvest. Either sow seed from one variety every two weeks from spring or do a couple of sowings of multiple varieties that mature at different times. Pinch out branching types to encourage sideshoots, but leave the single-stemmed ones alone.

TOP RIGHT: 'Velvet Queen'

IN THE VASE

Picking at the right stage is key to long vase life – you want to get to the blooms just as the petals start to lift off the face of the flower and before any insects have had a chance to get to them. If the flowers have already opened, as long as the petals are still facing forwards, you're okay. Doubles are the exception and need to be picked once the flower is fully open. Stripping off most of the leaves from the stem when conditioning will help extend vase life. I also like to use the flowers once the outer petals have started to fall off. I love the look of the dark centers in arrangements in late summer and early autumn. Expect a vase life of 7–10 days.

A WORD ON SAVING SEED

It's really easy to save sunflower seed, but make sure your plant is not a hybrid – the seed packet should tell you. Once the back of the flower head has changed from green to yellow, cut the stems and pick off the seeds.

Zinnias (*Zinnia*)

Zinnias were admittedly a slow-burn for me; they reminded me a little too much of gerberas. However, after devouring a few nursery catalogs and indulging in a significant overspend on seeds, I've been happily experimenting with a few that caught my eye, and I now have new firm favorites to add to my must-grow list of annuals.

MY FAVORITES

Z. elegans Benary's Giant Series – tall with sturdy stems and huge flowers with 13 colors to choose from. I particularly like 'Purple' with its large, fully double, bright pink-purple flowers. Height 35–47 in (90–120cm).

Z. elegans Queen Series – some stunning color combinations: 'Queen Lime' has lime flowers with maroon centers and 'Queen Lime Red' produces pale red/salmon/ tan blooms tinged with lime. Height 30 in (75cm).

Z. elegans Zinderella Series – scabious-type zinnias with multilayers of petals that give them a tufted look. 'Zinderella Lilac' and 'Zinderella Peach' are both lovely soft colorways. Height 30 in (75cm).

Z. elegans 'Polar Bear' – large heirloom zinnia with double, "dahlia-type" white flowers with a green tinge – an elegant beauty. Height 35 in (90cm).

Z. elegans 'Lilliput White' – from the Lilliput Series with their small, perfectly formed, pompom flowers – a soft white with a hint of green. Height 24 in (60cm).

Z. elegans Super Yoga Series – long-stemmed, large-flowered zinnias. 'Super Yoga Dark Red' is a rich velvety colorway. Height 35 in (90cm).

Z. elegans 'Pop Art White and Red' – double, cherry red-and-white speckled variety that's a new favorite. Height 24 in (60cm).

IN THE GARDEN

It's easiest to direct sow seed once the ground has warmed up – the zinnias will thrive on it. However, the slugs in my garden have the capacity to annihilate a whole batch of seedlings overnight so I start mine off indoors six weeks before the last frosts and grow them on until they are sizeable enough to have a fighting chance. The experts say you shouldn't do this as zinnias hate root disturbance, but I've never had a problem. Once the seedlings are up and off, it's important to pinch out the growing tips when the plants reach around 12 in (30cm), to encourage bushier growth (and more flowers). Keep picking and they'll keep flowering.

IN THE VASE

Harvest just before the flowers are completely open and they'll last 7–10 days in the vase.

OPPOSITE: 'Benary's Giant Purple' (bright pink/purple), 'Benary's Giant Wine' (deep pink/purple), 'Super Yoga Dark Red' (red), 'Queen Red Lime' (salmon), and 'Lilliput White' (white).

Cosmos (*Cosmos*)

The first cosmos I grew was the simple white form, *C. bipinnatus* 'Purity'.
I fell for the classic, daisy-like looks of the flowers on the seed packet, but
discovered pretty soon that the feathery foliage was something to celebrate,
too – it's a great way to pad out an arrangement while retaining a lightness.
Cosmos is also a plant that helps prettify the cutting patch – no matter how
much I seem to cut there are always still masses of flowers bobbing about.
There are now many more varieties available, some with the most stunning
color combinations and detailing on the petals, which look as if they have
been hand-painted.

IN THE GARDEN

These half-hardy annuals are ultra-productive – you'll be picking bucket-loads and they go on and on, until they are knocked back by the first frosts. I sow indoors four weeks before the last frost and plant out after frosts have passed. Cosmos need some support – netting secured horizontally works best – but if you're growing only a few plants a series of twiggy sticks will do the job. They make quite large plants so space 12 in (30cm) apart. Pinch out the growing tips when the plants are 8 in (20cm) high, to encourage them to produce more sideshoots. I pot into 2¾ in (7cm) pots.

MY FAVORITES

C. bipinnatus 'Antiquity' – burgundy to salmon flowers that turn to bronze as they age and take on a "faded" look. Height 24 in (60cm).

C. bipinnatus 'Candy Stripe' – white with pink stripes and splashes. Height 32 in (80cm).

C. bipinnatus Double Click Series – double frilly flowers available in a mix or single colors. I love the rich purple-red of 'Double Click Cranberries'. Height 35 in (90cm).

C. bipinnatus Fizzy Series – semi-double flowers with tufted centers. 'Fizzy Rose Picotee' has white flowers with a beautiful purple-pink edged outline that looks as if it's been hand-painted. Height 35 in (90cm).

C. bipinnatus 'Purity' – daisy-like, single, pure white blooms with yellow centers. Height 39 in (100cm).

C. bipinnatus 'Rosetta' – blush-pink and rose-colored blooms with an inner ring of tufted petals. They have an exquisite, hand-painted quality to them. Height 35 in (90cm).

C. bipinnatus 'Velouette' – white stripes on deep wine-red flowers. Height 90cm.

IN THE VASE

Harvest when the flowers are just about to open. Vase life is about seven days.

OPPOSITE, CLOCKWISE FROM TOP: A mix of cosmos growing in my cutting garden in mid-summer, including 'Candy Stripe'; 'Antiquity'; 'Double Click Cranberries'; 'Purity'.

Icelandic poppies
(*Papaver nudicaule*)

I'd been using these crinkled, papery beauties in springtime photoshoots for years (and paying through the nose for them before it occurred to me to give growing my own from seed a try). My hesitation was in part due to their reputation for being tricky. They certainly aren't the simplest, but they're perfectly possible, even for beginners.

MY FAVORITES

Champagne Bubbles Group – mix of orange, pink, bright yellow, and white as well as single colors. Height 20 in (50cm).

'Wind Song' – soft and muted shades of apricot, pink, orange, creams, and whites. Height 18 in (45cm).

IN THE GARDEN

❊ There's much debate about whether it's best to grow Icelandic poppies as biennials or annuals (although technically they are actually short-lived perennials), so try a couple of options and find which suits you best.

❊ One option is to sow the seed directly after the flowering season has finished, following the natural rhythm of the plant – you should get earlier and bigger flowers than normal, the following year. I've never done this as the risk of slug damage to emerging seedlings is considerable in my garden, so instead I treat Icelandic poppies as annuals and sow them in late winter under cover.

❊ They can be slow so use "primed'"seeds if you can, which have been treated with a special coating to help germination rates and speed. I put the seed tray on a heated mat, where it'll stay until the seedlings have emerged and developed a set of true leaves.

❊ Then it's time to pot them on into individual cells or pots. As they grow slowly, a 72-cell tray or a 2¾ in (7cm) pot will be fine. Throughout the process be gentle when handling seedlings – they don't like root disturbance.

❊ After about 6–8 weeks the young plants should have bulked up and be ready for planting out. Harden them off (see Hardening Off Indoor Seedlings, page 52) before planting and they should be flowering within about six weeks.

IN THE VASE

❊ Harvest regularly to keep the flowers coming. The ideal stage to pick is when the bud starts to crack and you can see colour.

❊ To prolong vase life, sear the stems in boiling water for 20 seconds or with a flame. If you recut the stems, you'll need to sear them again.

❊ Despite their ephemeral appearance, the vase life should be 5–7 days.

ABOVE: Champagne Bubbles Group.
OPPOSITE: 'Wind Song'.

Black-eyed Susan (*Rudbeckia hirta*)

For years I thought these no-fuss flowers only came in cheery shades of yellow and gold, but a few years ago I discovered a whole other glorious color palette of these velvety, daisy-like blooms including rich cherry and, more recently, muted, softer, almost pastel shades. These plants are repeat bloomers so keep picking and they'll continue kicking out masses of blooms from midsummer and right through until the first frosts.

MY FAVORITES

'**Sahara**' – beautiful mix of pretty, knocked-back, muted coppers, yellows, and pink. A perfect mix with coral and peach dahlias, which also flower up to the first frosts. Height 24 in (60cm).

'**Cherry Brandy**' – another favorite with deep red-wine blooms. Height 24 in (60cm).

'**Cappuccino**' – rich mahogany-red petals with their tips tinged with yellow – a good companion for sunflowers in mixed displays. Height 24 in (60cm).

IN THE GARDEN

I sow these half-hardy annuals eight weeks before the last frosts, leaving them uncovered as they need light to germinate, and then transplant the plugs out once there is little risk of frosts. A sunny spot is best, but they can take a little shade. You can also sow direct in spring.

IN THE VASE

Keep picking and you'll have blooms for 3–4 months. They are quite quick to turn the water foul, so add a drop of bleach to the vase water and change it every few days. Vase life is 7–10 days.

LEFT AND OPPOSITE: 'Sahara'.

The floral fillers

Whipping up mixed displays and bunches becomes a joy when you have a good range of flowers to play with. A floral filler bridges the gap (quite literally) between the focal and secondary flowers and the foliage to pad things out, soften, and add a little bit of texture. They are indispensable in the cutting garden.

LOVE-IN-A-MIST (*NIGELLA*)

A perfect filler plant with decorative stamens featuring on flowers held above a froth of feathery foliage that doubles as a secondary flower in smaller arrangements. It's a hardy annual, so super easy to grow. I'll do one sowing in autumn direct, with another in spring to follow on. Support the plants with twiggy sticks or horizontal netting. Hold back on picking all the flowers so the seed pods can develop. These are very successful when dried. Expect a vase life of around seven days.

N. papillosa 'Delft Blue' – white flowers with painterly streaks and dark purple stamens. Height 24 in (60cm).
N. papillosa 'African Bride' – pure white flowers with rich, deep purple stamens. The flowers develop into decorative dark-colored seed pods. Height 35 in (90cm).
N. damascena 'Albion Green Pod' – pure white flowers with bright green stamens that form green seed pods. Height 18 in (45cm).

CORNFLOWERS (*CENTAUREA CYANUS*)

Cornflowers, with their thistle-like blooms, are a rare sight growing wild in fields, but they thrive in a cutting garden. They are easy to please and immensely useful in the vase as a filler. Cornflowers need constant picking to keep flowering and require support – horizontal netting installed when the plants are small is the best option. Sow these hardy annuals in autumn. They prefer poor soil, so don't add any fertilizer when sowing or planting out. Vase life is 5–7 days.

'Blue Ball' – particularly stunning, classic, vivid blue cornflower. Height 30 in (75cm).
'Classic Magic' – mix of mauve to dark purple and soft pink with some almost black flowers – some have white tips. Height 39 in (100cm).

ABOVE, LEFT: 'Blue Ball'.
LEFT: 'Classic Magic'.
OPPOSITE, CLOCKWISE FROM TOP: *Nigella d.* 'Albion Green Pod', *N. p.* 'Delft Blue' and *N. p.* 'African Bride'.

ABOVE: Sweet rocket growing alongside 'Sutton's Apricot' foxgloves.

OPPOSITE: 'Electron Mix' and 'Alba' sweet williams used as a filler with peonies.

SWEET WILLIAMS (*DIANTHUS*)

Strictly speaking, sweet williams are short-lived perennials, but most people grow them as biennials. Dense clusters of up to 30 blooms per stem give off an exceptional, sweet, clove-like fragrance. They have a super-long vase life of about two weeks if you keep topping up the water.

D. barbatus 'Green Trick' – non-flowering form with vivid green tufts that make an excellent filler. Height 18 in (45cm).

D. barbatus 'Hollandia Purple Crown' – stunning mix of purple shades with white patterning.

D. barbatus 'Alba' – lovely, pure white variety. Height 16 in (40cm).

D. barbatus 'Sooty' – beautiful ruby-black leaves and purple, almost black flowers. Height 16 in (40cm).

D. barbatus 'Electron Mix' – perfect mix of pinks, purples, plums, and whites – all in one seed packet. Height 24 in (60cm).

SWEET ROCKET (*HESPERIS MATRONALIS*)

This may not be one of the first flowers you think to grow, but this biennial with clouds of flowers is immensely useful as a filler when there's very little else to use, and it will happily grow in part shade. Sweet rocket can be treated as an annual if started off early enough in the year. Expect a vase life of about 5-7 days. Height 35–47 in (90–120cm).

THE JOY OF TIMING

Don't be put off growing biennials just because they take a little longer to flower. Yes, it's a bit of a challenge to remember to sow them in midsummer, when so much else is going on in the garden, but it's worth it. When biennials do finally flower the following year, in early spring, there's very little else to choose from in the cutting garden.

BISHOP'S FLOWER (*AMMI VISNAGA & A. MAJUS*)

Both species are billowing and graceful members of the cow parsley tribe, with clusters of tiny white florets above fine, feathery, green foliage. In general, *A. visnaga* varieties tend to be slightly beefier and less willowy than those of *A. majus*, with umbels that are slightly darker green and more rounded. Plants need support – it's best to use horizontal netting. Expect a vase life of 7–10 days.
A. majus 'Queen of Africa' – specifically bred for professional use as a cut flower; the growth is strong and upright. Height 55 in (140cm).
A. visnaga 'Green Mist' – darker green, more rounded umbels. Height 47 in (120cm).

WILD CARROT (*DAUCUS CAROTA*)

D. carota 'Purple Kisses' is a chocolate-colored variety of wild carrot with a mix of shades from white and soft pink to dark burgundy. An absolute favorite – I never seem to have enough. Support the plants (horizontal netting is best). Sear the ends of the stems in boiling water for 30 seconds when conditioning. Vase life is around seven days. Height 32–39 in (80–100cm).

WHITE LACEFLOWER (*ORLAYA GRANDIFLORA*)

Its delicate, lace-like, flat flower head is made up of a cluster of tiny, pure white florets with the outer florets having elongated petals. Stake the plants with twiggy stems or pea sticks, and keep picking to extend the flowering season. Vase life: around 7 days. Height 24 in (60cm).

BEAUTIFUL UMBELLIFERS

Frothy, light, and airy, these umbellifers add texture and a lightness of touch that gives an ethereal quality to an arrangement. I wouldn't be without these three in my cutting garden. An autumn sowing will give you larger, stronger, more prolific plants that will be flowering by the following spring. A second sowing in spring will then provide flowers later in summer.

PHLOX (*PHLOX DRUMMONDII*)

A cottage garden classic with clusters of blooms that come in a rainbow of hues. Either sow direct once the soil has warmed up in spring or start off eight weeks earlier indoors. Pinch out the growing tip and keep picking to encourage more flowers.

P. drummondii 'Crème Brûlée' – interesting variety of annual phlox where each flower is a slightly different mix of color – varying from dusky pinks to peachy creams – some with a gentle wash of lilac. The flowers are arranged in clusters and give off a wonderful scent. Height 18 in (45cm)

TOBACCO PLANT (*NICOTIANA*)

From pure whites and soft pastels to green and deep purple, these trumpet-shaped, sweetly fragrant blooms are a varied bunch not only in color but also in stature; taller varieties such as *N. sylvestris* grow to 59 in (150cm) high. The tall tobacco plants look fantastic as hero flowers in large arrangements, but I find I use much more of the shorter varieties as a floral filler with the larger going unpicked in the garden. The only downside to these plants is that the stems are sticky and resinous. I grow mine under cover in early spring six weeks before planting out. They will last around seven days in the vase.

N. Avalon Series 'Avalon Lime/Purple' – stunning F1 variety with pink-purple shading to the petals and green centers. Height 8 in (20cm).

N. × sanderae 'Perfume Deep Purple' – F1 variety with rich royal purple blooms. Height 24 in (60cm).

PAINTED TONGUES (*SALPIGLOSSIS SINUATA*)

This half-hardy annual with sprays of beautiful, velvety, trumpet-shaped blooms is best started off under cover 6–8 weeks before the last frosts and planted out once there is little risk of frost. Pinch out the growing tips once they reach 4 in (10cm) high, to encourage bushy plants. Flowers should last about five days in the vase.

S. sinuata 'Black Trumpets' – almost black chocolate-maroon variety that has golden centers. It fades to a rich burgundy-brown with stunning veining detail on the petals. Height 20 in (50cm).

PINCUSHION FLOWER (*SCABIOSA ATROPURPUREA*)

Its wiry wiggly stems mean that the pincushion-like flower heads of this plant bob about beautifully. They add a little bit of quirk to an arrangement – I'll often tease out a few so that they sit higher than the other flowers to give a garden-gathered look to a bunch. Expect a vase life of about a week.

'Beaujolais Bonnets' – a short-lived perennial that I grow as an annual. Deep wine-red centers with paler ruffled outer petals and white stamens. Height 24 in (60cm).

'Black Knight' – a short-lived perennial that I grow as an annual. A darker version with some flowers coming as nearly black. Height 47 in (120cm).

'Fata Morgana' – creamy apricot-yellow, really unusual flowers. Height 35 in (90cm).

LEFT: *Phlox drummondii* 'Crème Bruleé'
RIGHT: Salpiglossis sinuate 'Black Trumpets'

ABOVE: Scabious Black Knight
LEFT: N. 'Perfume Deep Purple'

The climbers

The vigor of these mighty half-hardy annual climbers still impresses me; going from seed to a mighty 6-10 ft (1⅘–3m) high in a season, swamping the tallest of my willow teepees by the autumn. Snip a trail or two to bring a sense of movement to an arrangement – or drape a length along the center of a dining table for an instant floral table runner.

CUP-AND-SAUCER VINE (*COBAEA SCANDENS*)

The greeny-white bell-shaped flowers are highly decorative with a ruffle of bracts surrounding each flower and long stamens that dangle down like the filament in old-fashioned light bulbs. The blooms age to a magnificent hue of purple that gently fades. There is also a white (more a creamy green) variety 'Alba'. It's one to start off early undercover – as it won't start flowering until it gets to around 5-6 ft (1½–1⅘m). It's a large, flat seed that is best sown on its side to prevent it rotting. I grow the seedlings in 6 in (9cm) pots and then plant them out among my sweet peas in early summer after the frosts. Once the sweet peas become less productive and their flowers shorter stemmed (usually in late July/August), I cut them out (leaving their nitrogen-fixing roots in the soil), carefully untangling them from one another, and allow the cup-and-saucer to take over. It's a trick I learned from Arthur Parkinson (head gardener at the Emma Bridgewater Pottery) –and it's genius. Height 10 ft (3m).

NASTURTIUMS (*TROPAEOLUM MAJUS*)

I originally started growing nasturtiums as a companion plant in the vegetable patch to deter aphids and cabbage white caterpillars (which works like a dream by the way). Beautiful informal trails crept through my raised beds and tumbled over the edges, and I was able to snip surprisingly long lengths for the vase. Trailing or climbing varieties will grow up to 6 ft (1⅘m) tall and are best grown vertically, but most of the non-trailing types have a lax growth habit that will still provide you with plenty of cutting material. I plant non-climbing nasturtium seed direct at the ends of my vegetable beds in the same space I grow narcissi bulbs. Sown just as the leaves are starting to die back in late spring, they're up and off as I come back to clear the withered narcissi leaves. There are some unexpected colors available, as well as the usual yellow/orange. Expect a vase life of around 4-5 days – searing the stems helps.

'Milkmaid' – a soft creamy-yellow, the palest variety and as close to white as you'll get. Height 6 ft (1⅘m).

'Empress of India' – deep rich ruby-orange flowers with dark green leaves. Height 18 in (45cm).

'Ladybird Rose' – a dwarf variety at only 8-10 in (20–25cm) high, but the exquisite dusky-rose coloring with dark ladybug spots at the base of each petal. Height 10 in (25cm).

BLACK-EYED SUSAN (*THUNBERGIA ALATA*)

This was a new one for me this season. The common bright yellow variety never appealed to me, but then I came across 'African Sunset' in a seed catalog – a mix of apricot, red, and buff flowers with burgundy centers, and it has now joined my list of must-haves. It's a long-flowering half-hardy climber that keeps pumping out blooms until the first frosts. It needs support. Height 6 ft (1⅘m).

OPPOSITE, TOP LEFT: N. 'Milkmaid'.
OPPOSITE, TOP AND BOTTOM RIGHT: *Cobaea Scandens* 'Alba'.
OPPOSITE, BOTTOM LEFT: *Thunbergia alta*

3 Bulbs

Sleeping beauties

Bulbs are some of the hardest-working plants in my cutting garden and provide me with stem after stem of hero flowers, secondary flowers, and fillers right through from spring to winter – I can never have enough of them. I love the simplicity of their growth: the dormant bulb is self-sufficient; it contains all it needs to grow and flower for the coming season. Once you've tucked it up under a blanket of earth, you do nothing other than sit back and wait for the magic to happen.

BULB SUCCESS

✳ In general, bulbs like good drainage and full sun best, so if you're on heavy soil add plenty of small stones or sand on planting. A good rule of thumb is to plant the bulb at a depth of four times the height of the bulb. Remember, you are planting for cutting, not for garden display. Make the most of your space by planting in wide strips or blocks in beds and borders – not scattered in clumps as you might elsewhere in the garden. Such an efficient arrangement makes it easy to harvest, weed, and plant around or over.

✳ Some bulbs when left in the ground come back year after year, flowering bigger and better each season until they need dividing and replanting; narcissi, fritillaries, and ornamental onions fall into this category. Other bulbs such as tulips don't, and the second-year flowers are never as good as those in the first year. I treat these as annuals and replant new bulbs each year, thereby also getting the chance to change the varieties I'm growing. I've noted in the separate sections in this chapter the best treatment for each bulb.

✳ When harvesting the blooms from a bulb to be left in the ground to flower another year, you must be mindful of the plant's need to photosynthesize and therefore leave enough foliage on the plant for it to do this. I've noted cutting advice for perennial bulbs in the individual plant sections.

✳ If you are desperate to tidy up the messy foliage and reuse that space for other plantings once you've harvested the blooms, don't. Give the bulbs a chance to produce flowers the following year and be patient – the fewer the leaves or the smaller they are, the longer it will take for the plant to produce enough food. After the foliage has changed color, generally 6–8 weeks after picking the flower, it's safe to clear them.

OPPOSITE, CLOCKWISE FROM TOP LEFT:
Fritiillaria 'Meleagris'; Dahlia tuber, *Allium roseum*, 'Pink Perfection' lily, 'Woodstock' hyacinth, Tulip, *Fritillaria* 'Persica', *Ranunculus*, 'Sir Winston Churchill' narcissi, *Anemone, Narcissi* 'Paper Whites', *Allium hollandicum* 'Purple Sensation'.

Tulips (*Tulipa*)

Tulips are the ultimate low-maintenance flower – you plant the bulbs in late autumn or early winter and do nothing until you come to cut them the following spring. They are one of my favorite flowers for the cutting garden as they are so reliable and are available in stunning forms and colors that you just can't buy in stores. Each year, new varieties are introduced so there's always something new to try.

MY FAVORITES

From the fifteen different classes of tulips to choose from, these are the ones I find most useful in the cutting garden:

Singles – available in early and late varieties to extend the season. These are simple and elegant in form. My all-time favorite is 'Queen of Night'.

Doubles – come in early and late varieties. Often mistaken for peonies, this is the type of tulip I plant the most of and still can never have enough. I grow 'Uncle Tom', 'Mount Tacoma', 'Aveyron' and 'La Belle Époque' each year. I can't wait to try out 'Nachtwacht' this coming season.

Triumph Group – one of the largest groups of tulips, but I particularly like T. 'Res Favourite' and T. 'Flaming Flag', both bred to look like Rembrandt tulips with painterly flames and streaks and a nod to the 1600s' tulip mania.

Fringed Group – edged with a fine fringe, to give a frilly appearance. These tulips are great for adding texture to an arrangement. 'Curly Sue' is a beautiful deep aubergine with delicate fringing.

Lily-flowered Group – have an understated beauty. Their long pointed petals curve outwards at the tips to create a star-like shape. 'Claudia' has a white edge to its mauve petals, which highlights its lily shape.

Parrot Group – feathery and ruffled and so over the top that I've been asked if they're actually real. Favorites include 'Black Parrot', 'James Last' and 'Negrita Parrot'.

Viridiflora – streaks of green alongside the base color. 'China Town' is a pretty soft pink that goes well with spring blossom.

Multiheaded – bearing 2–5 flower heads per stem, they come up slightly shorter, but it doesn't matter – I display them cut short in a cluster of small bottles. A new favorite is blood-red 'Estatic', and I'm trying 'Belicia' this coming season.

THIS PAGE, CLOCKWISE FROM ABOVE:
The spring border in my vegetable patch –
a mix of tulips and narcissi;
'Negrita Parrot' (parrot);
'Rems Favourite' (Triumph);
'Claudia' (lily-flowered);
'Curly Sue' (Fringed).

OPPOSITE, TOP TO BOTTOM:
'Carnaval de Nice' (Triumph);
'Queen of Night' (single);
'Averyon' (Early Double);
'Estatic' (Multiheaded);
'Apricot Parrot' (Parrot).

IN THE GARDEN

Professional flower growers treat tulips as an annual and lift up the whole plant, bulb and all, when they harvest, because the flowers in subsequent years aren't really up to much (the method also gives the growers a little extra stem length). It feels terribly extravagant to pull up the tulips in your own cutting garden each year and plant afresh for the next, but I've learned the hard way and now don't bother keeping any of the tulips I plant for cutting. My bulk order of tulips is one of my luxuries – an annual ritual where I spend a few evenings pouring over the latest bulb catalogs, adding new varieties to my list of old favorites.

While we're on the subject of ordering, be sure to order early (in high summer) as the interesting varieties get snapped up, and you'll be so annoyed when these are all over everyone else's Instagram feed and not yours come spring! I time my delivery: tulips are the last spring bulbs to go in the ground, planted once the cold weather has set in, to help prevent tulip rust. They are better in storage with your supplier in the right conditions than at home with you, where there's a chance they might go moldy or soft and squidgy while they wait for their moment.

I plant tulips in wide strips or blocks – remember you're planting for cutting, not for garden display. It's easier to dig a trench to lay the bulbs in and then backfill, rather than dig individual holes per bulb. Tulips like well-drained soil so add some small stones or sand if you need to. Place the bulbs three times as deep as their height, planting them close together, but not touching – like eggs in an egg carton. Water in well and then sit back and wait for the magic to happen.

ABOVE: 'La Belle Époque' and 'Queen of Night' alongside narcissi in my vegetable garden.

WHAT HAPPENS IF I DO LEAVE TULIPS IN THE GROUND?

I've found that the blousier, more flamboyant tulips that appeal to me for cutting tend to come back so much smaller the following years that it's just not worth me keeping them. However, there are varieties that come back well and naturalize better than others. Darwin and Viridiflora types are most likely to flower for several seasons. Ensure there's enough drainage (add lots of grit at planting), position them deep enough (around 8 in [20cm] minimum) and leave at least two sets of leaves on the stem when picking, to allow the plant as much chance as possible to photosynthesize food for the following year. It's not a good idea to overplant the tulips with other plants as the bulbs need to get hot over summer and do not require any supplemental water (another reason I treat them as an annual – I need that space).

HOW LATE IS TOO LATE TO PLANT THEM?

I came across a small, forgotten bag of tulips at the back of the allotment shed a few years ago. It was mid- to late winter (early February) and, despite thinking they would come to nothing, I planted them. I was amazed at how well they did, albeit a little shorter and later than I would have expected. So even if you've missed the boat on the "ideal" planting time, as long as the bulbs are still relatively firm, it's worth giving them a try.

OPPOSITE: 'La Belle Époque'.

LEFT: Mint and salvia leaves and Geum 'Mai Tai' mixed with 'Averyon', 'Copper Image', 'The Artist' and 'Blumex Favourite' tulips and with a trail of weeping birch. OPPOSITE: The same tulips with copper beech leaves.

IN THE VASE

❋ Homegrown tulips are so superfresh that they're almost "squeaky." They have a long vase life of about ten days and age beautifully, drying and crisping to faded beauties.

❋ For the longest vase life, harvest just as the buds are beginning to color, but before they have opened.

❋ Wrap the stems in paper and tie with string, to hold the stems vertical, while they drink the water and to help keep the stems straight.

❋ Tulips are so versatile that they can be used in many different ways. I put the multiheaded varieties, cut short, in small bottles or bud vases to decorate a tight space like a mantel or a shelf, or set them down the middle of a dining table. A huge bunch of tulips looks so extravagant in a big, short vase, or you could make them the star of the show in a mixed spring bouquet and allow their natural movement to be showcased.

❋ Tulips keep growing after they have been cut, so bear this in mind when you're arranging a mixed bouquet and cut them slightly shorter (about ¾ in [2cm]).

❋ They also lean toward the light, so keep turning your arrangement each day if you want to stop them drooping. However, I personally love the graceful bends this trait creates.

Daffodils & narcissi (*Narcissus*)

ABOVE: 'Acropolis'

While in my main garden I prefer the more understated (and some would argue more tasteful) varieties such as N. 'Actaea' and N. *poeticus* var. *recurvus* to naturalize through the grass under the apple and damson trees, my cutting garden allows me to indulge in the blousier double and frilly varieties in the slightly more unusual colorways of peach, apricot, orange, and coral. The stems I pick in spring for the house, which fill it with the most amazing scent, are a world away from the archetypal yellow trumpet daffodils that flood the stores in spring. Instead, my homegrown bunches include peony-like doubles, pure whites with gently bobbing heads, and heavily fragrant multiheaded varieties with loose clusters of small blooms.

'Cheerfulness'.

'Delnashaugh'.

'Dick Wilden'.

MY FAVORITES

There are 13 different divisions or groups of narcissi with thousands of varieties. All are easy to grow with very little care, returning every spring and rewarding you with more flowers each year as they multiply in their numbers. The following are my favorites, a mix of single headed and double headed.

WHITE

'**Acropolis'** – double narcissi of pure white interspersed with small, orange-red petals that have a beautiful, luxurious, almost satin-like quality to them. This one is top of my list for a reason – its beautiful spicy scent. Height 18 in (45cm).

'**Obdam'** – ivory-white, fully double headed with gardenia-like flowers. Everyone who sees this in my garden falls in love. Height 16 in (40cm).

'**Calgary'** – pure white and double headed with a lovely light fragrance. It produces two flowers per stem. Flowers later in the season. Height 16 in (40cm).

'**Thalia'** – an heirloom variety (see page 142). Late, single-headed, snow-white trumpet with multiple flowers per stem. This looks beautiful naturalized in grass. Height 12 in (30cm).

FLAMBOYANT BICOLORED

'**Delnashaugh'** – bicolored, white double headed with frills of apricot-pink in the center. It has a gentle fragrance. Height 18 in (45cm).

'**Replete'** – pure white, double headed with reddish orange center petals and a good fragrance. Height 16 in (40cm).

A SHOW-OFF YELLOW

'**Dick Wilden'** – exactly what you would expect from a daffodil in terms of that vivid archetypal yellow but with a twist, literally, as the segments twist and curl to create almost a pom-pom–like bloom. Height 18 in (45cm).

'Sir Winston Churchill'.

'Obdam'.

'Acropolis'.

MAGNIFICENTLY SCENTED MULTIHEADED

'Sir Winston Churchill' – sturdy stems with double-white blooms flecked with saffron-yellow. The fragrance is intense. One of my absolute favorites. Height 14 in (35cm).

'Bridal Crown' – double white flowers with smaller yellow petals at the center. Strong, sweet fragrance. An heirloom variety. Height 14 in (35cm).

'Cheerfulness' – double white flower with yellow inner petals. Flowers later in the season. Height 14 in (35cm).

'Erlicheer' – white with primrose-yellow flecks to the blooms, which can sometimes appear in multiples of up to 25 heads per stem. Height 18 in (45cm).

'Geranium' – tall, strong stems with rounded white petals that have vibrant red-orange centers. Height 14 in (35cm).

FOR INDOORS

N. Papyraceus 'Ziva' (Paperwhites) – a non-frost hardy Tazeta group narcissi with clusters of sweetly scented blooms perfect for forcing inside in winter (see page 142). Height 16 in (40cm).

With nothing happening above ground during the bulbs' dormant period between midsummer and late winter, it makes sense to plan your plantings so that the valuable space is being used for something else.

Most of the narcissi I grow for cutting are planted down a long border in my vegetable garden, where I know they'll lie undisturbed and the dying foliage doesn't bother me. To maximize the space, the narcissi are over-planted with dahlias – a trick learned from cut flower guru Sarah Raven at her garden at Perch Hill, UK.

I plant the narcissi bulbs as normal in late summer (if they aren't already in), and then in late autumn or early winter, after the first frosts, I dig up some of my dahlias, divide the tubers, and overplant the daffodils. In spring, cut back a few of the daffodil leaves around the dahlia plants when the new growth emerges and protect plants against slugs.

Elsewhere in my garden, multiheaded narcissi varieties line the edges of the raised beds in my vegetable patch. I sow a few nasturtium seeds as the narcissi leaves start to die back and, by the time I come to clear away the leaves, the nasturtiums are up and running. The beds drain freely so there's no chance of the bulbs rotting if I need to water.

In the mixed borders in my garden, I plant taller, single-stemmed varieties such as 'Obdam', 'Calgary' and N. 'Acropolis' in among my roses. After the narcissi have flowered, the emerging leaves of the roses hide most of the mess of the dying leaves without taking too much of the sunlight from them (which would hinder the process of photosynthesis). Once the narcissi leaves have died back, I then plant seedlings of annuals such as love-in-a-mist or short grasses over the top in among the roses, to give me pickings in late summer.

❀ It's best to plant narcissi in late summer or early autumn, to give the roots a chance to really get going before winter sets in.

❀ A position with full sun is best, but they can take a little shade. Good drainage is essential, or the bulbs are likely to rot – add small stones and sand if your soil isn't well-draining already.

❀ Plant the bulbs a full three to four times their depth with a spacing of 4 in (10cm). If they are planted too shallow, the bulbs are encouraged to reproduce and create lots of smaller bulbs that will be too small to flower for years.

❀ Although little care is needed, a mulch of homemade compost or mushroom compost in spring will give the bulbs a boost, as will a high-potassium foliar feed once or twice after flowering before the leaves start to die back. (I use a good-quality, organic tomato feed.)

❀ Dig the bulbs up and divide them every four years – you'll know that it's time to divide when clumps start looking overcrowded and you notice a reduction in the number or size of flowers.

WHAT TO DO ONCE NARCISSI HAVE FLOWERED

If you haven't cut all the blooms already, deadhead any spent flower heads by snapping them off between your finger and thumb so that the plant doesn't waste energy creating seeds. As tempting as it is to get rid of that straggly tangle of leaves – don't. The foliage is hard at work, absorbing energy from sunlight, and through the process of photosynthesis creating food to allow the bulbs to flower again the following year. If you cut the leaves, your chances for flowers next year plummet – the same goes for braiding.

OPPOSITE: 'Obdam'

IN THE VASE

Ideally, pick the flowers when the buds have colored up, but haven't yet opened and there's a gentle curve to the neck (known as "goose-neck" stage). If you're unsure if it's ready, give the bud a gentle squeeze between finger and thumb – it should feel soft. If it's firm, leave it a little longer. You'll get up to a week in the vase from this point.

WATCH OUT FOR THE STICKY SAP

Narcissi ooze a milky sap that can be irritating, so use gloves when harvesting if you're prone to skin sensitivity. The sap will also shorten the vase life of other flowers. If you want to mix narcissi with other flowers, you'll need to cut the narcissi to the required final length and condition them separately, in water with flower food for 12 hours (if you can, change the water once or twice). Don't cut the stems again when arranging or you'll have to start conditioning all over again.

ABOVE: 'Acropolis' and 'Sir Winston Churchill' mixed with foraged foliage.
OPPOSITE: Just picked from the garden – condition the stems separately before arranging with other flowers.

Persian buttercups & poppy anemone (*Ranunculus asiaticus & Anemone coronaria*)

You might be slightly underwhelmed when you first see the shrivelled corms of Persian buttercups, as they look like tiny bunches of brown bananas that have been left to dry up and wither while those of the anemone look like a dried treat you might give to your dog. However, come spring, they'll be churning out stem after stem of swoon-worthy, tissue-like blooms. They both need the same treatment, and I grow them side-by-side, so I've bundled them together here, too. They are seriously swoon-worthy.

SOAKING & PRE-SPROUTING

Soaking and pre-sprouting sounds technical, but it's easy, I promise, and worth it as it speeds everything up by a few weeks and helps you weed out any duds in the process. Starting off with warm water, soak your anemones and Persian buttercup corms for about 12 hours – they will swell to almost twice their size.

Then lay them in a half-filled seed tray and cover with a mix of soil and vermiculite. Keep the soil moist but not soggy and check them regularly. I put them in my greenhouse on a heated mat, but I've also used the airing cupboard. Small white roots will start to form within a week or two. Once these are about ½ in (1cm) long, plant them as normal somewhere sunny with free-draining soil.

IN THE GARDEN

If you have hard winters, it's best to start pre-soaking and encourage sprouting in early spring and plant out after all danger of the ground freezing has gone (about a month before the last frost where I am). Persian buttercups and *Anemone coronaria* start flowering about 90 days later. Alternatively, in milder areas begin in early autumn and plant out with some protection from frosts – I use a low caterpillar tunnel and horticultural fleece. Autumn-sown plants are bigger and more prolific and flower in early spring rather than summer. Keep cutting Persian buttercups and *Anemone coronaria* and they'll continue flowering for about ten weeks.

RIGHT: *A.* 'Jerusalem Pink'

FAR RIGHT: R. 'Elegance Striato Bianco', A. 'Bordeaux' and A. 'Black and White'.

OPPOSITE LEFT: Pre-soaking Persian buttercups and Poppy anemones.

OPPOSITE RIGHT: Pre-sprouted Persian buttercups ready to be planted.

TO LEAVE OR LIFT?

After flowering, the corms can be lifted up and dried, then stored until the next season. Alternatively, they can be left in the ground permanently, but they'll need protection from frosts and the soil needs to be extremely well draining or the corms will rot off in a wet winter. I pull mine up and use the space to grow a crop of half-hardy annuals in their place.

IN THE VASE

Vase life is excellent – expect around ten days. Persian buttercup stems can go squishy (and stinky) in the water, so don't overfill the vase – just a few inches will be enough.

MY FAVORITES

RANUNCULUS ASIATICUS

The widely available standard form of *ranunculus asiaticus* is pretty and comes in a wide range of colors, but it's the newly bred varieties coming out of Italy that are the ones to track down. They are seriously swoon-worthy.

Elegance series – some take-your-breath-away varieties with large, ultra-full, peony-like blooms including 'Elegance Pastello' in a soft shade of apple-blossom pink; 'Elegance Striato Bianco' – creamy petals edged in burgundy; 'Elegance Cioccolato' with rich cocoa-brown, vintage-looking hues; and 'Elegance Viola' in a velvety burgundy. All are truly stunning and not widely available, so snap them up when you see them. Height 8–12 in (20–30cm).

Pon-pon Series – some of the most unusual, multicolored blooms, each one tinged with green with ruffled petals. As corms, they are difficult to get hold of, but are sometimes available potted up in garden centers. They are worth the eye-wateringly expensive price tag. Height 12–16 in (30–40cm).

'Café caramel' - unusual variety in shades of gold, terracotta and caramel. Height 10 in (25cm).

'Friandine Rose Picotee' – burgundy-edged petals in shades of apricot. Height 12–16 in (30–40cm).

ANEMONE CORONARIA

'Jerusalem Pink' – sumptuous, vivid violet-pink blooms. Height 10 in (25cm).

'Mount Everest' – pure white, ruffled double with a green center. Height 8–12 in (20–30cm).

'Bordeaux' – as the name suggests, a rich red wine velvety color. Height 8–12 in (20-30cm).

'Mistral Black and White' – white petals delicately tinged with soft pink near the center.

Fritillaries (*Fritillaria*)

This family of plants will bring something special to your cut flowers. From the large *F. persica* to the dainty *F. meleagris*, their bell-shaped blooms add a little quirk that's just on the right side of weird. Fritillaries are a dream to work with as they are just so beautiful and feel a little exotic. Some varieties do have a rather unpleasant, foxy, or animalistic smell, such as *F. raddeana* and, although beautiful, I prefer to enjoy those in the main garden.

MY FAVORITES

F. persica – tall spires of maroon waxy blooms, sometimes flushed with green that swoop down rather elegantly as they flower; 'Ivory Bells' is the white version that isn't really "white" but more of a beautiful creamy green. Height 32 in (80cm).

F. Meleagris – even though they are short at only 6 in (15cm), these nodding burgundy flowers with their distinctive checkerboard design are still one of my most prized harvests to use in arrangements. Also come in white. Height 6–12 in (15–30cm).

F. uva-vulpis – unusually colored petals: a combination of deliciously matte, almost suede-like, plum-brown dipped in yellow at the ends. Height 10 in (26cm).

IN THE GARDEN

The smaller varieties of fritillaries are unusual for spring bulbs in that they like damp – their ideal setting is a damp meadow or the edge of a damp woodland. The bulbs of the smaller varieties are good value so you can afford to indulge and be generous. The bulbs of *F. persica*, however, like well-drained soil so add plenty of small stones into the hole before planting. Take a bit of extra care when planting these large bulbs, setting them on their side, as there's a large hole in the middle of each bulb that can trap water and cause the bulb to rot. All like full sun or part shade.

IN THE VASE

They are great for adding a bit of quirk and a little something you just don't get from a standard florist's bunch. The tall spires give height and a gorgeous sense of movement as the stems twist and curl as they mature, while the smaller varieties add an element of the exotic. Pick when the bottom third of the flowers are open. All have a vase life of 5–7 days.

ABOVE: *F. persica* with white lilac
'Madame Lemoine', weeping birch
and *Geranium phaeum* var. *phaeum*
'Samobor'.
LEFT: *F. persica* alba.
OPPOSITE: *F. meleagris*.

Hyacinths (*Hyacinthus orientalis*)

For room-filling, knockout scent, nothing compares to hyacinths. In fact, some people find the fragrance a little too much of a good thing, so be careful where you position your vase – I tend to avoid my bedside. I don't grow masses, but I'll add 20 or so to my bulb order each year. I grow them at the edges of the borders in my cutting garden and also in pots to either bring into the house or arrange on our outdoor dining table so I can enjoy the view from inside. Most people think of hyacinths as classic blue or white, but there are some unusual colors available as bulbs that you'd struggle to buy as cut flowers.

IN THE GARDEN

Hyacinth flowers tend to be smaller and less dramatic from the year after planting. This is down to the bulb-producing bulblets, which drain the mother bulb and makes it smaller and smaller until it eventually stops coming up altogether. In an ideal world, the little bulblets would grow on and take over and bloom themselves, but in my experience it's just not worth waiting. I enjoy the first year's super-sized bloom and the smaller flowers that come in their second year, and then I pull them up and buy new bulbs.

In order to give your bulbs the best shot at reblooming, really well-drained soil is key. Add a handful of small stones when planting, for the bulb to sit on. When harvesting, you'll need to cut quite high to leave some leaves on the plant so it gets a chance to photosynthesize – this leaves them rather short, which is why I tend to use them as a potted arrangement.

MY FAVORITES

'Woodstock' – rich deep burgundy-maroon. Height 10 in (25cm).

'Apricot Passion'– a pretty, soft pink-apricot color. Height 10 in (25cm).

'Miss Saigon' – deep violet to lilac blooms. Height 10 in (25cm).

'China Pink' – soft vintage pink. Height 10 in (25cm).

'Dark Dimension' – the darkest hyacinth available – a lovely, deep, inky dark purple. Height 10 in (25cm).

'Jan Bos' – strong bright red-pink. Height 10 in (25cm).

IN THE VASE

✻ Pick hyacinths when one-third of the flowers are open and they'll last about a week. They can irritate the skin, so if you're prone to sensitivity, wear gloves when handling.

✻ Like most spring bulbs, they prefer cold water when conditioning.

✻ Hyacinths have a tendency to bend and twist in the vase – it's a natural part of their movement. I like to embrace it rather than trying to tame them.

OPPOSITE, CLOCKWISE FROM TOP LEFT: *H.* 'Woodstock' and 'China Pink' with narcissi and muscari. *H.* 'Apricot Passion'. *H.* 'Anna Lisa'.

Other spring bulbs

The classic heroes of the season – tulips, narcissi, ranunculus, and anemones – might be at the top of your list when ordering your spring bulbs, but there's magic to behold in some of the more delicate, miniature marvels that will bring you to your knees, quite literally.

LILY OF THE VALLEY (*CONVALLARIA MAJALIS*)

This diminutive beauty with the most delicious fragrance falls into my "plant-and-forget-about" category. Bury its rhizomes (or "pips" as they're known) in the soil and it just gets on with doing its thing. Come spring, shoots emerge to reveal green leaves, followed by flower spikes with tiny white bells on top of wiry stems. Lily of the valley is great for an area of the garden that's in part shade and is crying out for ground cover. Once it's settled in, it will romp away and you'll be rewarded with more and more blooms each year as it spreads. Harvest by pulling the flower stem away from the plant rather than cutting, to gain extra stem length. Vase life is 6–10 days.

C. majalis var. rosea – dusty-pink flowers. Height 12 in (30cm).

GRAPE HYACINTHS (*MUSCARI*)

These miniature marvels are best appreciated up close and personal where you can admire their tightly packed clusters of flowers and fragrance. They are super easy, and if they're in a well-drained, partly shaded spot, they'll come back year after year (another of my "plant-and-forget-about" beauties). Grape hyacinths come in the classic blue – from light to dark – but also in white and pink. If you pull the flower stems rather than cutting, you'll get extra length. Vase life is about a week.

M. armeniacum 'Alida' – large flowers of bright blue edged in white and a slightly longer stem than most. Height 8 in (20cm).
M. aucheri 'White Magic' – good white for cutting. Height 6–8 in (15–20cm).
M. 'Pink Sunrise' – delicate soft-pink blooms. Height 7 in (18cm).

RIGHT: *Convallaria majallis* var. *rosea*.
BELOW: *Muscari* 'Pink Sunrise'.
OPPOSITE: *M. armeniacum* 'Alida'.

Dahlias (*Dahlia*)

Dahlias went through a bit of a renaissance a few years ago and have emerged as one of the floral designers' favorites. A dahlia can give you everything from a cutesy pom-pom or a delicate, waterlily-shaped bloom to a weighty, densely packed flower head the size of a dinner plate. These plants come in almost every color imaginable: from vintage French-knicker pink, coral and peach to brooding, almost-black purples and velvety reds and everything in between. The enormous range in terms of color, size, and form means the choice can be immense. Dahlias are pretty much foolproof to grow in a sunny, well-drained spot. They are hardworking and generous – blooming in my garden just after midsummer, giving me bucket after bucket of blooms that keeps me in hero and secondary flowers right through until they are hit by the first frosts. They have to be my all-time favourite summer plant for the cutting garden.

When choosing which dahlias to grow, I think in terms of a family of colors that will work together in a range of sizes and different forms, to create an interesting mix in the vase. I'll choose two or three dinner-plate-sized blooms, a couple of medium ones and a few smaller ball or pompoms. That way, I've got all the flowers I need to create a mixed arrangement by just adding a few stems of foliage and filler if I feel the vase needs it.

MY FAVORITES

LILACS, PINKS, APRICOTS & ORANGES

'Café au Lait' – firm favorite with florists, with its huge blooms in a mix of pale pink, blush, and soft peach. Breeders have recently released a new generation including the gorgeous 'Café au Lait Royal', which has the same coloring as the original with some light pink coloring. Height 47 in (120cm).

'Shiloh Noelle' – exquisite, dinner-plate-sized variety with soft pink-white flowers gently colored with lavender-lilac. Height 47 in (120cm).

'Penhill Dark Monarch' – dinner-plate-sized, full blooms in varying shades of pink, from apricot right through to raspberry. Height 59 in (150cm).

'Jowey Winnie' – sophisticated, Ball-type dahlia in a knocked-back pink that's not too sugary. Height 39 in (100cm).

'Thomas Eddison' – 'Thomas Eddison' – dinner-plate-sized blooms in vivid plum/raspberry. Height 30 in (75cm).

'Labyrinth' – large flowers in varying shades of pink and peach. Height 35 in (90cm).

'Nicholas' – apricot dahlia with subtle markings of pink and a darker crimson center. Height 35 in (90cm).

'Zippity Do Da' – cute little pom-pom–type dahlia with mauve to pale lilac-pink flowers. Perfect for bud vases. Height 35 in (90cm).

WHITE & CREAM:

'White Perfection' – classic white dahlia with large blooms. Height 47 in (120cm).

'Platinum Blonde' – pretty anemone-type dahlia with white outer petals and a mass of cream inner florets that create a pincushion effect. Height 39 in (100cm).

'White Linda' – soft white blooms with lavender centers. Height 59 in (150cm).

THE BROODING TYPES: DEEP PURPLES, REDS & BURGUNDIES

'Downham Royal' – ball-type dahlia the perfect size for mixed bouquets. It's a rich velvety purple. Height 43 in (110cm).

'Kenora Macop-b' – with spiky edged petals. A long-time favorite. Height 47 in (120cm).

'Black Jack' – deep chocolate-red with large flower heads of velvet petals – a semi-cactus type. Height 43 in (110cm).

ABOVE: 'Kenora Macop-B', 'Thomas Eddison' and 'Edge of Joy' dahlias with cosmos, wild carrot, and copper beech. The stems are supported with chicken wire.

GETTING THE MIX RIGHT

When choosing which dahlias to grow, I think in terms of a family of colors that will work together in a range of sizes and different forms to create an interesting mix in the vase. I'll choose two or three dinner-plate-sized blooms, a of couple of medium ones, and a few smaller ball or pom-poms. That way, I've got all the flowers I need to create a mixed arrangement by just adding a few stems of foliage and filler if I feel it needs it.

INTERESTING MARKINGS

'Edge of Joy' – elegant dahlia from the Decorative Group. White flowers with beautiful painterly strokes of purple. One of my current favorites. Height 35 in (90cm).

'Crème de Cassis' – medium-sized flower heads with petals that have a light pink upper side and darker pink-plum underneath, which gives it a painterly feel. Height 43 in (110cm).

'Mick's Peppermint – unusual dahlia with large, white-pink blooms that are streaked and flecked with crimson and raspberry. Height 47 in (120cm).

'Marble Ball' – mauve, ball-type dahlia speckled with burgundy. Height 35 in (90cm).

IN THE GARDEN

❋ Buy dahlias as bare-root tubers or as small-rooted cuttings in spring, to plant out after the last frosts. After purchase, cuttings need to be grown somewhere frost-free to bulk up, while tubers can either be planted out just before the last frosts with some protection or started off in pots a month or so before, to get a head start on the season. They will have formed bushy plants by the time the last frosts have gone and they are ready to plant out.

❋ Dahlias are hungry feeders, so add plenty of home-made compost (a 4–5 in [10–13cm] layer) to the soil each spring before planting dahlias with some organic fertilizer. I plant them relatively close together at a spacing of about 24 in (60cm) apart.

❋ Dahlias need support, so I use hazel sticks or bamboo canes and string to create a sort of "cat's cradle" around the stems of each plant. Once the plant is growing up and away, you won't see any of the support material.

❋ Slugs love nothing better than gorging on the young shoots of dahlias, so watch out for the first signs of growth and protect the shoots. Every other week, I apply a homemade tea of comfrey (see page 55).

❋ I pinch out the main growing tips on plants when they reach about 12 in (30cm) high, to encourage more flowers. Aim to pinch above the fourth set of leaves. Pick a sunny day to do this so that the hollow stem you've exposed doesn't fill with water and increase the chances of rotting.

❋ Don't cut back or lift a dahlia until the very end of the growing season. Tubers will be getting bigger and better underground right up until the first frosts grind the process to a halt.

TO LIFT OR NOT TO LIFT?

There's much debate about whether to lift the tubers or leave them in the ground and mulch, because dahlias aren't frost hardy. I actually do both. For years I lifted the tubers each autumn, but the year I had my twin boys – born just at the time I would normally lift the tubers – I didn't get around to the job and they stayed in the ground over winter, protected with a thick layer of mushroom compost that I'd managed to get on. The following spring almost all came up, completely unaffected. I now leave the majority of my dahlias in the ground, digging up some as insurance in case of a particularly bad winter and lifting those I want to propagate. Whether or not this will work for you depends on how cold and wet your winters are and on how well-drained your soil is. It might be worth experimenting and leaving a couple in the ground, hedging your bets for the first few winters to see if it works for you.

HOW TO LIFT & STORE

If you're going to lift your dahlias, it's best to wait until they've had a few frosts – their leaves and stems will blacken. Shorten the stems, then dig the plants up. Go carefully – it's very easy to prong the tubers with the fork if you go too close. Trim off any small roots and take off as much of the soil as you can. Then cut the stems to about 6 in (15cm) long and lay them out in trays or wooden boxes upside down to dry for a week or so somewhere frost-free. Then turn them right side up and cover the tubers with peat-free compost, but leave the crowns exposed. Store in a dry, frost-free place – I put my dahlias in a garden shed. If extreme cold is forecast, I cover them with a breathable, old cotton rug to protect them. Check on the tubers during their dormant period and lightly water if they begin to shrivel. Come spring, divide the tubers and replant.

OVERLEAF, LEFT: A section of my dahlia patch with 'Smoots', a vivid pink dahlia, growing in the foreground. OVERLEAF, RIGHT, CLOCKWISE FROM TOP LEFT: 'Shiloh Noelle', 'Mick's Peppermint', 'Marston George', 'Marble Ball', 'Zippity Do Da', 'Smoots', 'Mick's Peppermint', 'White Perfection', 'White Linda' 'Zippity Do Da', 'Marble Ball', 'Labyrinth', 'Downham Royal', 'Café au Lait' (center).

CLOCKWISE FROM TOP LEFT: 'Labyrinth' with 'Ida Gayer' in the background, 'Edge of joy', 'Jowey Winnie', 'Platinum Blonde', 'Black Jack', 'Nicholas', 'Thomas Eddison' and 'Penhill Dark Monarch'

INCREASING YOUR PLANTS

Dahlia tubers aren't particularly expensive and offer a great return on your investment, but costs can mount up if you want to indulge in lots of different varieties. Fortunately, it's very easy to propagate dahlias and increase your stock, from cuttings or by division.

BY CUTTINGS

✤ To propagate dahlias from cuttings, start the tubers off in late winter in pots somewhere light and frost-free – I put them on a heated bench in the greenhouse. I leave the top third or so of the tuber uncovered with soil so it's easy to see the top of the tubers and take the cuttings.

✤ Before long, you should have lots of healthy shoots to take cuttings from. Select a strong shoot about 3 in (7½ cm) long and, using a sharp knife, slice it away from the mother plant. Ideally, you want to take a bit of the tuber with you as this increases the chances of rooting (this is known as a basal root cutting).

✤ Remove the lower leaves and cut any large ones on top in half, to reduce the stress on the cutting.

✤ Dip each cutting into hormone rooting powder and pop the cuttings at the edges of a small square pot filled with free-draining compost (I add vermiculite to store-bought,

peat-free compost) and set in a propagator. If you don't have a propagator, insert a few sticks in the soil and cover with a clear plastic bag; then seal with an elastic band.

BY DIVISION

Clumps of dahlias can be split into many individual tubers readily. Use pruning or a knife to divide the large clump first in half, then into individual tubers. You need to make sure that each tuber has at least one "eye" (like the ones you see on potatoes). I wait until spring to divide mine as it's easier to see the "eyes" once they start to swell and go red at the beginning of the growing season.

IN THE VASE

✤ Harvest when the flowers are fully open, as dahlias are one flower that doesn't continue to open post-harvest.

* Compared to other cut flowers, dahlias have a relatively short vase life, but if you put the stems into a bucket of cool water straight after cutting, and let them rest somewhere cool, vase life can be extended to around five days.

* Some people sear the ends in water or recut the stems under water after the initial harvest cut, as it's said to prevent the chance of airlocks in the stems.

ABOVE, LEFT TO RIGHT: Start dahlia tubers off early in pots to propagate. Once shoots reach about 3 in (7½ cm) they make good cuttings. A tiny amount of the tuber is taken along with the cutting.
ABOVE LEFT: The cuttings quickly develop a strong root system.
ABOVE RIGHT: When dividing, make sure each piece of dahlia tuber has at least one growing point or eye.

Lillies (*Lilium*)

It was their epic fragrance that first made me want to grow lilies, but they looked so magnificent in the garden that I couldn't actually bring myself to snip them just as they were coming into their prime, no matter how good they smelled. I now grow them mostly in pots to bring inside to watch their trumpets bobbing in the breeze from an open window and enjoy that gorgeous, sweet perfume as it wafts about. I steer clear of the Asiatic and Oriental lillies as they are so cheap to buy in supermarkets that there's no point paying for pricey bulbs. Instead, I grow one or two of the more unusual modern hybrids and focus mainly on the classic beauties that look like they've just been plucked from a romantic pre-Raphaelite painting.

MY FAVORITES

L. candidum – madonna lilies are pure white with smaller flowers than many other lilies. They prefer neutral to alkaline soil and need planting close to the surface, so you can just see the tops of the bulbs above the soil. Slightly earlier flowering than the others. One of the trickier lilies to grow. Height 3–6 ft (1–1⅘m).

L. martagon – Turk's cap lilies have purple-pink petals peppered with black that curve back on themselves (hence the name). This species can appear rather delicate, with its 2 in (4cm)-wide blooms, but don't let looks deceive – it's quite robust. It prefers pH6.5–7.5 soil and is at home in a light woodland; it will naturalize if happy once established. Height 3–5 ft (1–1½m).

L. regale – one of the easier species to grow, the pink buds open to reveal white petals shaded with purple-pink on the outside and a beautiful shade of yellow on the inside. Super-scented, they are absolutely glorious to have in the garden and the house. Prefers a humus-rich, well-drained soil of pH 7.5. Height 59 in (150cm).

L. r. 'Album' – is a pure white form that has a gentle shading of yellowy green on the outside and a warm buttercup-yellow glow on the inside. Height 47 in (120cm).

L. Pink Perfection Group – stunning purple-pink trumpet lily with a stronger purple on the outside of the flower. It's become my new favorite. It's not fussy about soil pH and is one of the easier lilies to grow. The Pink Perfection lilies pictured are in their first year in my garden and are yet to fulfil their mighty potential. Height 5 ft (1½m) or more.

L. 'Lankon' – it was love at first sight when I came across this hybrid of *L. longiflorum* and *L. lankongense* at the RHS Chelsea Flower Show a few years ago. The white petals have beautiful gentle markings that look like they have been sprayed, spattered, or lightly dusted with deep purple, each one unique. They aren't fussy about soil pH. Take care as these lilies come up early in the season and new growth may be damaged by frosts. Height 3–6½ ft (1–2m).

OPPOSITE: Pot-grown *Scabiosa atropurpurea* 'Beaujolais Bonnets' with weeping birch in crate arrangement.

RIGHT: *L. regale.*
BELOW: *L. martagon.*
FAR RIGHT: *L.* 'Lankon'.

IN THE GARDEN

❋ Lily bulbs are quite an investment so it's worth taking care of them as best you can. A sunny spot is good, but some can take part shade, although they like to be drier rather than wet. The bulbs will rot if the ground is waterlogged so make sure you plant in soil that is free-draining and rich in humus.

❋ Also check what soil pH your lilies need – some prefer acid while others like alkaline. Generally, lilies need to be planted with about 6 in (15cm) of soil above (*L. candidum* being the exception, see My Favorites, page 130). They aren't the easiest flowers to grow in the ground – they can be ravaged by ground slugs and rot in a wet winter. If you add the dreaded lily beetle into the mix, it may mean you have to replace your bulbs after a few years. I've had more success growing lilies in pots using a good soil-based compost with added small stones. If there's an extended period of extreme wet weather in winter, I'll move my plants under the eaves of the shed, where they'll be in the rain shadow of the building.

❋ Some of the taller lilies will definitely need support. I do this with a few willow sticks and twigs from prunings from the garden – the leaves on lilies are strappy and won't be enough to camouflage something unsightly.

❋ To give my lilies the best chance I give them a seaweed feed a few times after they've started into growth in spring. Always deadhead the flowers after flowering, so they don't waste their energy producing seed. A quick snap between finger and thumb should do it. In autumn, I cut the stems to ground level once they've turned brown and apply a mulch. If you have heavy soil or wet winters, you are better applying the mulch earlier in the season.

The dreaded lily beetle makes a beeline for lilies (and also fritillaries) and shouldn't be ignored. Squash these small red beetles when you see them, otherwise they'll munch through the foliage, and the attack may result in undersized bulbs developing that won't flower the next year.

HARVESTING & CONDITIONING

If you are going to cut your lilies rather than use them as a potted display, make sure to leave a good portion of the stem with its leaves intact on the plant – cutting no more than about a third of the stem length, or half on the taller varieties. This does mean shorter flowers for you, but the plant needs to keep those leaves to photosynthesize food to flower the following year. The flowers don't need any special treatment when conditioning and should last in the vase for over a week.

A WORD ON POLLEN

Most lilies have prominent stamens with anthers on the top that bob about and become covered in bright yellow pollen once open. This is great for the bees, not so good for your furnishings or your clothes as it can stain quite badly. To solve the problem, you can pick off the anthers before they open, pinching them between finger and thumb. If you do get some pollen on fabric, don't get it wet or try to rub it with your fingers – use a pipe cleaner or a piece of sticky tape to dab the pollen off gently.

Ornamental onions (*Allium*)

I grow a few different ornamental onions in various situations in my garden: the classic pom-pom *A. hollandicum* 'Purple Sensation' is massed in drifts that float among the perennials; and the football-sized *A. cristophii* are wonderful along one of the borders. I'll pick them all for the vase, but prefer to use them once they've formed their seeds – either while still green or after they have turned brown and dried. The larger-flowered varieties with densely packed pom-pom flower heads can be rather difficult to use in a mixed arrangement, as they can be quite domineering and tend to take over. Instead, for cutting I grow varieties with more petite flowers or a more relaxed form, and snip these in their prime in early summer.

MY FAVORITES

A. schubertii – large, spiky dark pink flowers that are often likened to a firework. Even though it has a big flower head – around 12 in (30cm) across, it's very useable and adds a great texture and sense of movement to a large arrangement. It's also brilliant dried. Height 16 in (40cm).

A. cristophii – another one that looks great dried. Flower heads are about 8 in (20cm) across. Height 24–35 in (60-90cm).

A. 'Spider' – a new variety very much like *A. Schubertii* (see above), but in a deep purple and on a slightly smaller scale. Height 12–16 in (30-40cm).

A. neapolitanum Cowanii Group – pure white flower heads, about 2 in (5cm) across, make this very useable in smaller bouquets. Height 12 in (30cm).

A. 'Roseum' – looks similar to *A. neapolitanum* Cowanii Group (see above), but in a pretty soft pink. Height 24 in (60cm).

Nectaroscordum siculum – this ornamental onion has recently been moved to a different genus. It has bell-shaped, hanging, greeny white flowers tinged with reddish brown. An absolute must for me. Height 32 (80cm).

A. nigrum – white ornamental onion with green, bead-like ovaries at the center of the each flower head. The flower head isn't a full pom-pom, but a dome shape. Height 24 in (60cm).

A. sphaerocephalon – a late-flowering ornamental onion with egg-shaped, purple flowers that are immensely useful in arrangements. Height 24–35 in (60-90cm).

IN THE GARDEN

Ornamental onions are great value as they flower for ages, look interesting when in seed, and dry brilliantly. They are easy to grow – plant the bulbs in autumn in a sunny position and if they're happy they'll naturalize well. Good drainage is key; add extra small stones or sand at planting if your soil is heavy.

IN THE VASE

As a member of the onion family, ornamental onions have a distinct oniony smell when the stems are cut or crushed. Harvest when about half of the florets are open. To help minimize the oniony smell, change the water regularly. Ornamental onions have a vase life of more than a week.

OPPOSITE: CLOCKWISE FROM TOP LEFT: *A. cowani, A. Schubertii, A. Nectaroscordum siculum, A. sphaerocephalon,* A. Purple Sensation hollandicum.

Gladioli (*Gladiolus*)

Gladioli are the flamboyant extroverts of the cutting patch – their towering spikes of funnel-shaped blooms can reach over 3 ft (1m) high and come in some rather bold color combinations. I prefer the slightly more restrained colorways that showcase the velvety texture of the petals. Gladioli are a fantastic way to create a large display from summer right through to autumn.

MY FAVORITES

'**Espresso**' – sultry, deep crimson. Height 47 in (120cm).

'**Indian Summer**' – unusual dusky peach-coral gladioli. Height 47 in (120cm).

'**Plum Tart**' – rich magenta-purple. Height 47 in (120cm).

'**The Bride**' – very pretty, delicate-flowered gladioli that flowers later in summer – pure white and understated. Height 16–24 in (40–60cm).

IN THE GARDEN

❈ Gladioli are not fussy about soil type, but need a well-drained, sheltered spot in full sun. They take about 90 days to flower from planting and come all at once, so to spread your harvest plant the corms every three weeks rather than in one big batch.

❈ The corms aren't hardy so need to be dug up before the first frosts and kept somewhere that's frost-free over winter. This is actually really easy – just pull up the corms once the leaves start to yellow and turn brown, shake off the excess dirt, then snap the stems away from the corms. Keep the corms somewhere dry and cold (but frost-free) over winter.

❈ You might see baby bulblets (also known as cormels) form around the mother bulb. Pull these off and plant in small pots and grow. They will take a year, maybe two, to flower.

RIGHT: 'Espresso' in the garden – the florets appear on only one side of the stem – you can't tell which side when you are planting – so it's just luck which way they'll face.
OPPOSITE: 'Plum Tart' with branches of copper beech and weeping birch in an early autumn display.

IN THE VASE

❈ Harvest when the bottom two gladioli flowers start to open.

❈ Keep at least four leaves on the plant when cutting if you want to reuse the corms.

❈ Some people pinch out the top of the flowering stem to encourage the unopened flowers on the stem to bloom, but I don't mind that they never open so I never bother.

❈ They have a good vase life of more than a week.

LEFT: Acidanthera.
BELOW: Star of Bethlehem.
OPPOSITE: 'The Pearl' Tuberose with 'New Look' dusty miller and bishop's flower.

Other summer, autumn & winter bulbs

One of the joys of growing your own cut flowers is the luxury of choosing to grow a bloom for its sheer beauty without having to consider how viable it might be commercially – you only have yourself to please. Search out off-the-beaten-track bulbs that might never make it to a florist's shop to bring something unique to your arrangements.

TUBEROSE (*POLIANTHES TUBEROSA*)

Tuberose has the most heavenly scent – a sweet gardenia-like perfume that might be too heavy for some, but is one that I love to wallow in. I've found the bulbs take a little coaxing to get into flower their first year and need a certain level of pampering to rebloom again. However, as the bulbs are expensive to buy, I've always thought them worth the extra effort. Old-fashioned tuberose have single blooms, but I prefer the doubles.

The best chance of success is to give the corms plenty of sunshine and heat – I grow mine in pots in the greenhouse. They need a long growing period to bloom; start them off early indoors, to get ahead on the season. Give them a regular balanced feed that's not too heavy on nitrogen. Harvest when most of the flowers are open around 80 percent. The reluctance to rebloom is due to the mother bulb expending its energy creating little baby bulbs rather than bulking up to rebloom (it dies off in the process). It can take up to three years for these babies to flower. There's a vase life of about five days.

'The Pearl' – much showier flowers. Height 24–35 in (60–90cm).

'Sensation' and 'Pink Sapphire' – both double, soft-pink varieties. Height 28–32 in (70–80cm).

ACIDANTHERA (*GLADIOLUS CALLIANTHUS*)

These elegant, gently drooping, pure white flowers with purple blotches at their centers have the most exquisite fragrance and make the perfect cut flower. They are surprisingly cheap to buy, so I always feel I can afford to be generous and plant lots. The flowers appear in late summer or early autumn. Inhaling their fragrance as it wafts about the garden is a bittersweet reminder that we're on the cusp of autumn, and that summer will soon be over.

Acidanthera like it hot, so plant the bulbs in free-draining soil in full sun at the start of summer. This tender bulb isn't frost hardy and should be lifted after the leaves have yellowed (see *Gladioli*: In The Garden, page 136) and stored over winter in a frost-free place before being replanted the following spring. Height 30–35 in (75–90cm).

STAR OF BETHLEHEM (*ORNITHOGALUM ARABICUM*)

This often-overlooked bulb has clusters of sweetly scented, star-shaped, white flowers with black centers, which bloom from late spring to summer. It is a hardy bulb and as long as your soil is free-draining it will happily come up year after year, eventually forming clumps that will produce more and more flowers each year. Cut the flowers once the lower florets open. The bonus is that the flowers have an extremely long vase life, easily lasting a couple of weeks. Height 20 in (50cm).

SUMMER SNOWFLAKES (*LEUCOJUM AESTIVUM*)

The multiple nodding, bell-shaped, white flowers on each stem look as if someone has taken a fine paintbrush dipped in green paint to the tip of each and every petal. Summer snowflakes are closely related to snowdrops (see below) but are the taller, slightly later-flowering option with wider flower heads – although their flowering periods overlap in my garden. I always find summer snowflakes bloom in late winter or early spring, and not in summer as the name suggests. It's a truly unique addition to your cutting garden that will come back year after year and slowly spread. Cut the flowers just before the buds open. Expect a vase life of around five days. Height 16 in (40cm).

The spring snowflake (*L. vernum*) is earlier flowering than summer snowflake, slightly shorter at 12 in (30cm) and bears just one flower head per stem. Both prefer moist but not waterlogged soil.

SNOWDROPS (*GALANTHUS*)

Snowdrops might not be the first plant you think of for the cutting garden, and I'm not suggesting that you take up precious space in your flowerbeds with rows of them, but if you have a part-shaded spot in your garden – under a tree or among some grass – they are ideal. You can just plant and forget about them while they multiply and spread. When there's very little else going on in the garden, snowdrops are a joy to behold – a handful of these diminutive beauties – their delicate blooms tipped with green – always manages to cheer me in the depths of a long winter. When we bought the cottage, I was lucky enough to inherit hundreds of snowdrops among the grass, and since redesigning the garden I've re-homed swathes of them. They are best moved (and introduced) into your garden just after flowering, when "in the green" – that is, just before their leaves start to die back, as they establish better than dry bulbs. Cut the flowers just before the buds open. Expect a vase life of 2–3 days.

G. nivalis f. *pleniflorus* 'Flore Pleno' – particularly pretty, double variety with green-tipped inner petals. Height 12 in (30cm).

RIGHT TOP AND BOTTOM:
Snowdrop 'Flore Pleno'
OPPOSITE: Summer snowflakes
with *Garrya elliptica* catkins and
foraged foliage.

Forcing bulbs

With the cutting garden deep in slumber and so little going on outside in the garden in terms of flowers, my floral displays in winter are built around bulbs that can be forced, that is, grown outside of their normal flowering season.

MY FAVORITES

AMARYLLIS
I don't grow amaryllis to cut, as the bulbs are more expensive than buying the stems as a cut flower. Instead, I grow them to use as potted displays. They are often available cheap at markets already potted up in winter – the downside is the varieties are limited. If you are buying the bulbs dry, you'll get much more choice. The bulbs can be kept after flowering, given a rest period and then brought back into flower the following year.

'Magic Green' – ivory-white with a green center with burgundy painterly markings. Height 18 in (45cm).
'Apple Blossom' – pure white with pretty pink veining. Height 24 in (60cm).

NARCISSI
I pot up big bowls of these in succession to see me through winter. The classic variety for forcing is *Narcissus* Paperwhite 'Ziva' (height 16 in [40cm]) or *N.* 'Tête-à-tête' (height 6 in [15cm]), but pretty much any of the *N. Tazetta* varieties will work. Paperwhites aren't hardy – I take them out of their pots, dry and store them, and then repot them the following year in late summer or early autumn. The hardy varieties can be planted out in the garden (at four times their height).

HYACINTHS
Planting these in pots is my favorite way to enjoy hyacinths, as I feel they get lost in the garden. You get to appreciate them up close when they're in a pot on a table. Prechilled bulbs are available in a wide range of colors. My favorites for inside are *Hyacinthus orientalis* 'Woodstock', which is deep burgundy-maroon, and the classic mix of blue and white such as *H.o.* 'Delft Blue' and *H.o.* 'White Pearl'. Height 10 in (25cm).

TOP: Individual pots of amaryllis 'Rapido' arranged in a bowl – the trails of *Pilea glauca* help to camouflage the pots.
ABOVE: *Narcissus* 'Thalia' is also a good variety to force over winter.
OPPOSITE: Potting up hyacinth and narcissi bulbs.

HOW TO FORCE BULBS

❀ Buy "prepared" hyacinth bulbs, which are prechilled so that the bulbs will flower outside their normal season. The chilling tricks each bulb into thinking it's already been through winter and it's over a little sooner. Bulbs that originate from warm climates (such as amaryllis and paperwhite narcissi) don't need a cool period to trigger them to bloom.

❀ For hyacinths, a wide, shallow pot works best as the bulbs don't need to be planted deeply – the top of the bulbs can be just under the surface of the soil with a minimum of about 3 in (7 ½ cm) soil beneath the bulbs. Narcissi like a little more root run, so give a deeper container. Amaryllis is best planted in a pot just marginally bigger than the bulb. You can group these smaller pots within one larger one, for more impact.

❀ Use a well-draining soil mix. If your container doesn't have holes, add a few handfuls of small stones or sand to the soil and be careful not to overwater. If you're using a bowl from the house, line it with plastic first to prevent it becoming damaged.

❀ Hyacinths and narcissi look best when they are clustered together, so set them closer together than you would in the garden. Once potted, give them a good water. For decorative purposes, I use florists' moss to cover the bare soil when I'm potting smaller bulbs.

❀ Narcissi and amaryllis need to be positioned somewhere warm such as a sunny windowsill, but the hyacinths should go somewhere cold with a period of dark so that the flowers don't start to come out while the plants are too short. Pop the planted hyacinth container in a black plastic bag and put it somewhere unheated, such as a shed or garage. Hyacinths need a period of 8–10 weeks there before being brought into the house and the light. They should then flower in 3–4 weeks. Once the plants start to come up, I push twiggy sticks from the garden into the pots or containers, to support the stems.

❀ I'll often skip the whole forcing process given here and insteasd buy pre-potted bulbs when I see them during winter at a good price at the market. I'll then keep the bulbs in their individual pots and nestle them together in a container with some trailing house plants to hide the pots – or I'll add moss to cover everything.

4 Perennials, Shrubs & Trees

Adding the magic

When designing a cutting garden, it's easy to become sidetracked by the vast range and instant return that annuals and bulbs can give. You could build your whole cutting garden around just annuals with a smattering of bulbs, and with a bit of planning you'd have blooms from spring to autumn. However, it's your choice of perennials, shrubs, and, if space allows, trees that you incorporate into your arrangements that will set your flowers apart – they add the magic and allow you to create out-of-the-ordinary displays. Plant the right shrubs and perennials and they'll work as hard for you as any annual or bulb. Some are admittedly fleeting beauties, such as peonies, but there are others that flower for an extended period or give you more than one flush of blooms; you can be picking repeat-flowering roses and hydrangeas from summer all the way into autumn.

GROWING TIPS

❋ **Get them off to a good start**: Prepare the ground well, incorporating plenty of well-rotted organic matter and improving drainage if needed. Perennials and shrubs will be in the ground for a number of years, so it's worthwhile making them a good home.

❋ **Treat your plants as a crop:** If you're going to include perennials and shrubs in your cutting garden (as opposed to squeezing a few more in an existing bed), remember that you are growing for harvest, not for display. Plant in rows or blocks so that you're able to pick and tend the plants efficiently.

❋ **Extend your season:** Most perennials that are suitable for cut flowers bloom during spring and summer. By choosing varieties of the same plant that flower at different times, you'll be able to extend their flowering season: there are early, mid- and late season peonies, for example. It's possible to trigger some perennials to produce a second flush of flowers later in the season by cutting them hard back to the ground after their first flowering: lupins and delphiniums fall into this category.

❋ **Feeding and watering**: Some shrubs and perennials are hungry plants (such as roses and delphiniums). If you're expecting these plants to perform and produce top-quality blooms, you'll need to keep them well fed and watered throughout the season. I use a liquid tomato feed every couple of weeks during their growing season, along with a little liquid seaweed, and I mulch thickly in autumn or spring.

❋ **Pruning**: Growing perennials and shrubs isn't high maintenance, but it's not without work. Along with the feeding and watering, you need to be aware of any pruning regime required for each plant. Most herbaceous perennials are easy; generally, they are cut back hard to the ground after they die back in late autumn.

❋ **Increasing your stock**: Perennials and shrubs are expensive to buy, but they are easy to propagate by dividing established clumps in autumn or spring, or by taking cuttings (the timing depends on the type of cutting and the plant). It's also much easier to grow perennials from seed than many people think. Sow the seed along with your biennials in midsummer and they'll be ready to plant out in the garden in early autumn (or can be overwintered in the greenhouse). If the packet says the seeds need a period of cold before germination, just pop the seed packet in the freezer for a couple of weeks before sowing. Some perennials flower in their first year when started off early in the year, under cover.

SEE ANYTHING AS FAIR GAME

If you already have an established garden, you may be growing perennials that are suitable as cut flowers. If you're wanting only a few stems every now and then, you just need to alter your mindset to allow yourself to raid the borders for the vase occasionally. Anything is fair game. If you like the look of something, snip a stem and try it out. There are very few plants that aren't worthwhile cutting, in terms of vase life.

ABOVE: A section of my perennial border with roses, peonies, lupins, phlox, and salvia.
LEFT: Buckets in early summer filled with cutting-garden classics like roses and peonies, but also wild foxgloves, bellflowers, and astilbe, which also make great cut flowers.

Roses (*Rosa*)

It was the rose that kick-started my obsession with homegrown blooms. I was blown away by the beauty of *Rosa* 'Yves Piaget', a vivid pink rose with knockout scent that I saw in a top florist's shop in Paris. After a while spent online playing detective, by winter I was planting three bare-root bushes that formed the beginnings of my first cutting garden in my tiny London garden.

SELECTING ROSES

Garden roses have a more relaxed and graceful growth and are less stiff than the upright, modern, imported ones. Many roses for the cut flower industry have had their scent bred out of them so that they can be transported from Kenya, Ecuador, and Colombia, where they are grown on an industrial scale. Things are getting better with more and more local flower farms popping up and choosing to grow stunning, scented blooms, but nothing beats the thrill of selecting and growing your own beauties.

Look for repeat-flowering roses that produce blooms again and again through the season. The variety is enormous, from the range of color to form. There are singles, doubles, shallow cups, chalice shapes, to name just a few. Some roses are formed in clusters at the end of upright stems, others grow in sprays along gently arching stems. Bear growth habit in mind when choosing your plants – they're not just about the flowers; each rose has a different personality that will make it more or less suitable for the space you have.

Then there's the fragrance. I urge you to go to a garden with a decent collection of roses to make your choice in the flesh, burying your nose among the petals, noting any that stop you in your tracks. When selecting roses for your cutting garden, choose blooms that you find irresistible, but check whether they last in water – not all do. I grow lots of roses in my garden. While not all have been specifically chosen for cutting, they still don't escape my flower snips. Some just don't last, no matter how well I condition them. It's sometimes less than a day before I hear the gentle tumble of petals on the table, but that doesn't stop me cutting them and enjoying them.

Most of the roses I grow in the cutting garden are highly scented English roses bred by UK grower David Austin or by the French breeders Meilland; I also add a few modern floribunda roses and hybrid teas to the mix. They have proved to be good performers in my garden, where they repeat bloom through the season.When picked at open bud stage, roses will last 3–5 days in the vase.

ABOVE: Enjoying floral leftovers in my potting shed.
OPPOSITE: 'Hot Chocolate' roses – the color changes dramatically as the flowers age – from orange to a rusy red-brown.

ABOVE: 'Boscobel'.

ABOVE: 'Burgundy Ice'.

MY FAVORITES

THE REDS & DEEP PURPLES

'Munstead Wood' – deep crimson to purple, velvety, sumptuous blooms with a strong fragrance. Bred by David Austin. Height 39 in (100cm).

'Burgundy Ice' – stunning floribunda rose that's free-flowering throughout the season. Beautiful burgundy velvety blooms. Height 35 in (90cm).

'Hot Chocolate' – floribunda rose with an unusual coloring, starting off as orange, then turning to a rusty red-brown. Has a light fragrance. Height 35 in (90cm).

THE YELLOWS, ORANGES & APRICOTS

'Lady of Shallot' – I grow this beauty as a climber – it can easily put on 71 in (180cm) of growth in a season. Its orange-red buds open to orange blooms that soften in color as they age. It has lovely scent and healthy vigorous growth. A David Austin rose. Height 95 in (240cm).

'Lichfield Angel' – creamy-white shrub rose with apricot hues, a light clove scent and stunning fully double, deeply cupped flowers. Height 59–95 in (150–240cm).

'Duchess of Cornwall' – hybrid tea rose with coral-apricot flowers that have an old-fashioned rose look and a spicy perfume. Height 35 in (90cm).

'Wollerton Old Hall' – yellow buds with flashes of red open to chalice-shaped, butter-yellow blooms that soften to cream with apricot and peach. Heavily perfumed. Another winning David Austin rose. I grow this as a

ABOVE: 'Wollerton Old Hall'
TOP: 'Duchess of Cornwall'

ABOVE: 'Munstead Wood'.   RIGHT: 'Yves Piaget'.

ABOVE: 'Tranquility'.

climber in the middle of my perennial borders. Height 59–95 in (150–240cm).

THE PINKS

'Queen of Sweden' – exceptionally pretty, shallow-cupped rose in soft pink with a light scent. Growth is upright and very healthy. A David Austin rose. Height 35 in (90cm).

'Yves Piaget' – one of my all-time favorites and the rose that started my obsession. It is a deep pink with an intense rose fragrance and frilled edges to the petals. Bred by French growers Meilland. Height 35 in (90cm).

'Princess Alexandra of Kent' – strong, warm pink with deep cups and a fruity fragrance. A David Austin rose. Good resistance to disease. Height 39 in (100cm).

'Boscobel' – another shrub rose with the most extraordinary coloring that goes from rich salmon to deep pink and all the shades in between as blooms age. A vigorous and healthy grower. Height 35 in (90cm).

THE LILACS, SILVERS & BUFFS

'Harry Edland' – dusky lilac floribunda rose with the most divine classic rose fragrance. Height 32 in (80cm).

'Blue For You' – floribunda rose that's an impressive repeat flowerer – born on clusters. Light fragrance. Height 30 in (75cm).

'Koko Loko' – an unusually colored rose – each flower being a slightly different shade, starting off as tan-buff, then turning to a soft lilac-silver pink. A light fragrance. Height 30 in (75cm).

THE WHITES & CREAMS

'Tranquility' – perfect creamy-white blooms that open with a hint of greeny yellow at their centers, but age to a pure white. Light fragrance on this shrub rose. Bred by David Austin. Height 59 in (150cm).

'Winchester Cathedral' – fully double, sweetly scented, white blooms that sometimes have a touch of pink at their centers. Height 47 in (120cm).

BELOW: 'Queen of Sweden'.

LEFT: 'Princess Alexander of Kent'.   BELOW: 'Harry Edland'.

LEFT: 'Blue for You'.
ABOVE: 'Wollerton Old Hall'.

IN THE GARDEN

Planting: It's best to buy roses in their dormant season as bare-root plants to go out in the garden between late autumn and early spring – bare-roots are much cheaper than container-grown plants, there'll be many more varieties available, and they'll get off to a flying start. Prepare the ground really well before planting and use mycorrhizal fungi to help the root system develop for an even healthier plant.

Feeding: I mulch with manure or compost after pruning in late winter, to improve the quality of the soil. Feeding is essential if you want the plants to keep producing blooms through the season. I use a specialist foliar feed for roses (Uncle Tom's Rose Tonic), which I spray at the start and end of the season; it's high in potassium. Once the flowers start coming, I apply a seaweed feed or homemade comfrey tea (see page 55) each week.

Watering: Roses need watering during dry periods and this is best done at ground level with a hose, instead of from overhead.

Pruning: At the end of the season before winter weather sets in, I give my roses a light prune – cutting back about one-third of the plant. This helps prevent wind rock, which can damage the plants. Then, in late winter, I prune my roses hard to 12–16 in (30–40cm) from the ground, leaving about four or five main stems. Prune at an angle just above an outward-facing bud so the water can drain off and not sit in the bud. Any diseased, damaged, or dead wood needs to be cut back in the process, as you would with any pruning. Cutting back hard like this encourages long stems to grow, for cutting. Keep picking and deadheading through the season to encourage more blooms.

BELOW: One of the rose beds in my cutting patch. Narcissi bulbs are planted in among the rose bushes. Once the bulb foliage dies back in late spring, I'll plant young hardy annuals like love-in-a-mist to grow among the roses.

RIGHT: There's always room for another rose. This 'Madame Alfred Carriere' is growing against my potting shed.

GROWING FOR HIPS

I'm lucky enough to be able to plunder hedgerows overflowing with rose hips in autumn, right on my doorstep. The roses in my cutting garden are either cut in bud for the vase or deadheaded to prolong the flowering season – they never get a chance to set hips. There are roses that are grown specifically for their hips (see page 219).

A WORD ON BLACKSPOT

The dreaded scourge of the rose is a fungus that infects the leaves with ugly black spots before turning them yellow and causing them to fall off completely. The best way to avoid blackspot is to choose varieties that are disease resistant in the first place, so they are better equipped to fight it. Keep your plants as healthy as you can so they aren't stressed and are strong enough to fight, and be diligent about getting rid of any infected material that will harbor the disease. That means disposing of all infected leaves at the end of season (don't compost them) and cutting away any old wood as it can hold the spores over winter, ready to reinfect new growth in spring.

IN THE VASE

❋ It's best to harvest when the flower is still in bud, but the calyx (the green outer bit) is just opening.

❋ Because roses are very sensitive to being out of water, take a bucket filled with water out with you, to pop the stems into straight away. Keep them out of water as little as possible when handling.

❋ When arranging in the vase, retain the leaves on the top third of the stem as this helps the full color to develop and the petals to open, but, as usual, take off any that will be sitting underwater.

❋ I tend to arrange most of my roses in tight clusters in low vases. I love the density of color and scent this gives me.

❋ It's possible to revive a wilted rose if you get to it in time by recutting the stems at a slight angle, then "searing" the stems in just-off-the-boil hot water for 20–30 seconds. Protect the flower heads so they don't steam (see page 229).

ABOVE, LEFT: Just two foraged stems of a rambling rose twisted back on themselves fill this urn.
BELOW, LEFT: 'Koko Loko'.
OPPOSITE: An early-summer mixed display of 'Blue for You' and 'Harry Edland' roses with scented stocks, sweet williams, basil, and wild carrot.

Peonies (*Paeonia*)

On paper, peonies shouldn't be at the top of my list to grow for cutting because these large herbaceous perennials take up a lot of space for their 3–4 week window of flowering. However, these blousy blooms pull on my heartstrings, and so practicality goes out the window. The fact that patience is required – it can take about three years, sometimes five, for them to be sizeable enough to harvest from, makes your first generous armful all the more glorious. Did you know that peonies are exquisitely perfumed, too? This is a fact that is often overlooked as we go nose-first into the garden roses.

There are three different types of peonies: herbaceous ones, which die back to ground level each winter; tree peonies, which have woody stems that remain above ground the whole year; and intersectional (Itoh) hybrids, which are a cross of the two. I grow all three, but here I'll be focusing on the widely available range of herbaceous peonies, mostly the *P. lactiflora* cultivars that are so brilliant for cutting.

As much as I find the delicacy of single peonies charming, I don't grow them for cutting, as the ones I've tried just don't last in the vase. I've been told that *P. lactiflora* 'Pink Dawn' holds up well, but I have yet to try it. Most of the double peonies should last more than a week in the vase. If you're planting a few peonies, it's worth thinking about flowering times by selecting a mix of early, mid- and late season flowerers. In doing so, it's possible to extend the short season.

ABOVE: Mixed sweet williams cut short with 'Sarah Bernhardt', 'Red Charm' and 'Karl Rosenfield' peonies.

THE WHITES

P. lactiflora 'Gardenia' – pure white, sometimes with a hint of blush. The scent is magnificent. Early to mid-season flowering. Height 34 in (85cm).

'P. lactiflora Duchesse de Nemours' – highly fragrant, old variety with a little hint of greeny yellow when fully open. Early season flowering. Height 35 in (90cm).

P. lactiflora 'Festiva Maxima' – center petals have red flecks; each flower is unique with large outer guard petals. Good fragrance. Mid-season flowering. Height 39 in (100cm).

P. lactiflora 'Vogue' – free-flowering plant with white doubles that open to the palest blush pink before returning to white as it matures. Mid-season flowering. Height 34 in (85cm).

P. lactiflora 'Shirley Temple' – large blooms opening to a pale blush that fades to pure white. Heavy-bloomer. Mid-season flowering. Height 35 in (90cm).

THE PINKS

P. lactiflora 'Sarah Bernhardt' – a lovely soft pink; although widely available in the stores, it's still a thrill to pick my own. A very useful variety as it flowers later in the season and is a heavy-bloomer. Height 39 in (100cm).

P. lactiflora 'Karl Rosenfield' – bright crimson petals with prominent golden stamens and beautiful bronze-colored leaves in autumn. Mid- to late season flowering. Height 32 in (80cm).

THE REDS

P. lactiflora 'Red Charm' – a deep blood-red with a very interesting Japanese form, in which large guard petals surround a tightly packed center made up of petaloids instead of stamens. Early flowering – good to extend the season. Height 35 in (90cm).

P. 'Buckeye Belle' – another luscious deep-red peony, but semi-double in form with rich golden stamens that contrast beautifully with the petals. Early flowering. Height 35 in (90cm).

THE CORALS

P. 'Coral Charm' and 'Coral Sunset' – chameleons of the peony world. Both are semi-doubles that start out salmon-pink, with *P.* 'Coral Charm' being a slightly lighter shade, and fade to a beautiful soft peach via all the shades in between. Both early season blooming. Height 35 in (90cm).

IN THE GARDEN

❊ The best way to buy peonies is during the dormant season as bare-root plants – look for suppliers that state they send their orders out with at least three or four "eyes'"(growth buds) as they produce flowering-size plants relatively quickly – within a season or two of planting. You'll have to wait a little longer than that to pick, though

❊ Peonies like a sunny position in neutral to slightly alkaline soil with good drainage, but they can handle light shade. Don't let them dry out while they are establishing themselves.

❊ I actually do very little in terms of caring for my peonies – apart from cutting the stems back to the ground in autumn and giving them a mulch with fresh compost in spring. Unless your soil is poor, you shouldn't need to do anything more, either.

❊ However, you need to stake the plants as the huge blooms become so heavy the stems start to droop. A triangle of bamboo or sticks with a web of garden twine running between them will be enough to keep the peonies upright and will be hidden once growth gets underway.

A NOTE ON MOVING

Ignore the old wives' tale about not being able to move peonies. It's perfectly fine to do so – and autumn is the best time to do it. I've moved my current collection three times with no problems whatsoever. Often the reason for a plant not flowering post-move is that it has been replanted too deeply. The "eyes" – where the new growth comes from – need to be sitting just below the surface, covered by no more than 2 in (5cm) of soil.

OPPOSITE, CLOCKWISE FROM TOP LEFT:
'Karl Rosenfield'; 'Coral Sunset'; 'Coral Charm',
'Red Charm'; 'Buckeye Belle'.

BELOW: 'Shirley Temple' (white), 'Sarah Bernhardt' (pink) and crimson 'Karl Rosenfield' (crimson).

OPPOSITE, CLOCKWISE FROM TOP LEFT: 'Shirley Temple', 'Duchesse de Nemours' and 'Vogue'.

HARVESTING & CONDITIONING

❋ The best stage to cut peonies is at what growers call the "marshmallow" stage: gently squeeze the flower between your finger and thumb and if it feels like a soft marshmallow, it's ready. If it's more like a marble, leave it and check again in a few days. On doubles, this picking stage will be when the buds are just starting to open. Cutting at the marshmallow stage will give you more than a week in the vase.

❋ When picking, don't remove more than one-third of all the plant. Choose between stem length or quantity of flowers – if you want more flowers, pick shorter stems. Longer stems? Pick fewer flowers. I tend to gather short stems and use lots of them closely packed together in one vase or else in singles or threes in a cluster of smaller vases. Growing your own allows you the extravagance of having a plentiful supply to do this without the guilt of getting rid of all that stem length you pay for when you buy them from a florist.

❋ Some peonies produce more than one flower per stem. The leading flower bud is the biggest, with normally two others produced on sideshoots lower down. I extend my harvest by cutting the leading flower off first, then coming back for the others another day.

❋ The leaves of peonies are a useful foliage but be mindful of the plant and its need to photosynthesize. I wait until later in the season to pick the foliage as it's safer for the plant at that stage and, rather conveniently, is also when the leaves look their best, having taken on autumnal hues.

❋ Peonies are able to absorb water via their petals as well as the stems – for the best conditioning submerge the stems in a bath overnight.

ABOVE: *H. paniculata* 'Limelight' plays hero in this mixed display alongside bells of Ireland and various grasses.

ABOVE, RIGHT: Unknown varieties picked from my dad's garden drying indoors.

RIGHT: *H. macrophylla* 'Sweet Cupcake'.

Hydrangeas (*Hydrangea*)

Hydrangeas are possibly one of the hardest-working plants going, with some blooming from early summer right through to winter. They are the chameleons of the garden and offer an enormous variety in terms of color, with varying shades even on the same plant as their colors change through the season. Hydrangeas also continue to fade and age beautifully once cut.

MY FAVORITES

I've focused here on my favorites for the vase, from the mophead types (*H. macrophylla*) with their giant pom-pom flower heads and their quirky trait of changing color depending on your soil (more on this on page 164), to *H. arborescens* ones with their delicate, dome-shaped heads and the conical blooms of *H. paniculata* types. All are large deciduous shrubs.

In terms of the colored mopheads, as I garden on neutral to alkaline soil, I go for the pinks – personally preferring to wait to pick until the blooms mature and take on their late-summer colors with hints of greens and purples. The *H. arborescens* types flower on new growth, so if there's any frost damage over winter, you'll still get flowers. Some growers deliberately prune back hard in spring, to get larger flowers (but fewer of them), but I've found the flower heads become a little too heavy for their stems and they end up lolling about and flopping over, especially after rain, so I tend to stick with cutting to the first set of strong buds as I do for the mopheads. Prune paniculata hydrangeas in early spring by cutting back the previous season's growth to within a few buds of the woody framework.

H. macrophylla 'Madame Emile Mouillère' – magnificent, pure white-flowered mophead with a really long flowering period. The blooms start out as white-green then become tinted with pink (more so if grown in sun) as the flowers age. You can pick these flowers from early summer right through to autumn for use in wreaths. Height 79 in (200cm).

H. macrophylla 'Sweet Cupcake' and 'Elegant Rosa' – both compact with floriferous, strong stems and very pickable shades of pink all the way through the season. Height 3 ft (1m) – both compact at around 39 in (100cm).

H. macrophylla 'Mathilde Gütges' – stunning blue if you garden on acid soil and will flower in shades of violet-blue to purple-blue. Height 59 in (150cm).

H. arborescens 'Annabelle' – large, snowball-like globes of creamy-white flowers that look a little like my springtime favorite *Viburnum opulus* (see Flowering shrubs, page 188). Height 98 in (250cm).

H. arborescens 'Incrediball' – similar to 'Annabelle' (see above), but with bigger flowers and bred specifically with tougher branches to help the flowers stand up. I am yet to try this cultivar. Height 59 in (150cm).

H. arborescens 'Sweet Annabelle' and *H.a.* 'Ruby Annabelle' – recent additions to the Annabelle Series, both favorites in my cutting garden as their flowers start out a raspberry-pink and fade beautifully through summer before taking on the most exquisite green hues later in the season. When left unpicked, their skeletal flower heads take on a sculptural quality in winter – it's real take-your-breath-away beauty at every stage. Height 47 in (120cm).

H. paniculata 'Limelight' – dense, conical-shaped flowers in large clusters that start out lime green in midsummer, fade to cream, then become flushed with pink and finish a deep pink. Height 59 in (150cm).

IN THE GARDEN

❄ Hydrangeas are pretty easygoing plants – they love well-drained, moist soil that isn't too quick to dry out and prefer part shade. Blooms can be burnt from too much sun exposure, so somewhere that gets morning sun but is shaded in the afternoon is perfect.

❄ However, although hardy, new growth can be damaged by hard frosts in spring so avoid exposed, east-facing sites and position plants somewhere sheltered out of the reach of cold winds.

❄ Hydrangeas need very little care to keep them flowering well. Lots of organic matter added to the soil on planting will get them off to a good start, and a generous annual mulch of well-rotted leaf mold, garden compost, or manure will give them the boost they need.

❄ Keep an eye on them if it's a really hot summer – they'll begin to wilt a little if they are too dry, but they'll soon perk up after a good watering.

❄ Other than that already mentioned above, and deadheading, very little pruning is required to keep hydrangeas blooming. As you'll be cutting the blooms for the house, you'll be doing even less.

ABOVE: *H. arborescens* 'Sweet Annabelle' picked in late summer once it has taken on autumn colors with sunflowers (stripped of their petals) and copper beech foliage.
OPPOSITE: Foraged autumnal foliage alongside *H. arborescens* 'Sweet Annabelle'.

A WORD ON SOIL PH & COLOR

Mophead hydrangeas change color (except the white ones) depending on the pH of the soil: the more alkaline it is, the pinker the flowers; the more acidic, the bluer they will be. While it's perfectly possible to adjust the pH of your soil to grow blue flowers on alkaline soil, by adding aluminium sulphate, and pink blooms on acid soil by adding lime, it's something I've never had the urge to do. If you do, bear in mind it's something that will need to be maintained – the color change isn't permanent, and it may affect neighboring plants if they can't tolerate the new soil conditions. It might be better to grow the hydrangeas in large pots, where the soil conditions can be more easily controlled with imported soil.

ABOVE: Mophead hydrangeas picked from friends' gardens conditioning in the bath.
OPPOSITE: A mix of autumnal mophead hydrangeas picked at the perfect stage for drying.

HARVESTING & CONDITIONING

✳ Hydrangeas are prone to wilting, so they need a little special treatment. The key is really in picking the flower at the right stage of maturity – newly emerged flowers don't last as long as the older ones.

✳ Always bring a bucket of water out to harvest and put the stems straight into water after cutting.

✳ Remove most of the leaves (all would be ideal) as this gives each flower the best chance of staying hydrated.

✳ Condition the flowers by plunging them right up to their necks (just below the flower heads) in water with added flower food, and put them somewhere cool and out of direct sunlight for 12 hours. If it's a warm day, I'll drape some wet paper towels over the heads as an extra measure. Alternatively, you can give cut hydrangeas a bath in cold water overnight. This also helps to revive them if any start to wilt after you arrange. (Some florists rave about using alum powder – dipping the just-cut stems in the powder before conditioning, but I have yet to try this.)

✳ Recut when you come to arrange the hydrangeas, and keep them out of direct sunlight. Mist the flower heads each day if it's particularly warm, to help prevent drooping.

HOW TO DRY HYDRANGEAS

I find the best way to dry hydrangeas is to arrange them in a vase indoors with 1–2 in (3–5cm) of water. The water will gradually evaporate, allowing them to dry gently and not lose too much color. This works for me nine times out of ten – the key is to pick the flowers at the right stage; they need to be mature and feel a little papery if you cup your hand over the top. Alternatively, you can leave the flower heads on the plant to dry if you have a dry late summer or early autumn. However, prolonged rain will turn the flowers brown before they've had a chance to dry properly.

Hellebores (*Helleborus orientalis*)

The joy of growing hellebores is that they flower when little else is going on in the garden. While winter is still at its worst, their buds burst through and their gently nodding heads catch you by surprise. Hellebores are rarely available to buy as a cut flower and eye-wateringly expensive when they are, so they're one of my absolute must-grows. Despite their delicate appearance, they are incredibly easy to grow – they fall into my "plant-and-leave-pretty-much-alone" category. Once you've tucked them up in a sheltered shady spot with rich soil, there's very little you have to do other than add a layer of compost around the plants each mid-winter.

Plants are expensive and take a few years to mature and get into the swing of pumping out flowers, but they are worth the wait. From frilly doubles to speckled singles in colors ranging from bruised purples and aubergine to acidic greens and chartreuse to the softest mottled peaches and pinks – there's something to suit all tastes. Each individual plant will also shift colors dramatically over its flowering period as it matures: changing, for example, from off-white to blush pink to acidic green, which is part of their magic.

If you're ordering an unnamed variety it's a bit of a lottery as you can't be sure what color you're going to get. If you can, buy plants when in flower so you can see exactly what they'll be like in terms of color and pattern.

IN THE GARDEN

❋ Hellebores thrive in a sheltered spot, planted into free-draining soil. Don't let them sit in waterlogged soil or they'll rot. The ideal place is at the outer edges beneath the canopy of a deciduous tree or the shady spots among mature shrubs in a mixed border.

❋ Check under mature plants in spring for seedlings – hellebores can be tricky to grow from bought seed, but self-seed readily if left to their own devices. Gently re-home any seedlings you find into pots and grow outdoors in a shady part of the garden before transplanting to their final position in the garden in autumn. They will take a few years to bloom, which goes some way to explaining their high price.

❋ Although evergreen, leaves can start to look shabby, so I cut back the foliage in mid-winter as the first signs of growth appear. New leaves will form shortly afterwards. It's at this point I apply a layer of compost around the plants as a mulch.

OPPOSITE: Mixed *H. orientalis*, foraged blossom, catkins and birch twigs.

ABOVE: *H. orientalis* and *Fritillaria meleagris* with spring blossom, hornbeam, and hawthorn.
LEFT: A particularly fine hellebore with an 'anemone' center.
TOP LEFT: *H.* x *hybridus* 'Blushing Bride'.
OPPOSITE: *H. orientalis* at varying stages of growth. To extend vase life, harvest once the stamens have fallen and the tiny seed pods have started to form.

HARVESTING & CONDITIONING

As tempting as it is to harvest the flowers when they have just opened and are in their full glory, exercise a little patience if you can – vase life will be limited otherwise. Wait until the stamens have dropped (stamens are the little strands at the center of the flower that carry the pollen) and the seed pods have started to form. You'll get much longer from your blooms then – often two weeks or longer when cut at this point.

However, if you're anything like me, you won't be able to help yourself from picking some hellebores while in full bloom (and to my mind, at their most beautiful), so proper conditioning is vital, otherwise they'll droop within 24 hours. Dipping the stems in 1–2 in (3–5cm) of boiling water for 30–60 seconds helps the blooms last a little longer. Do this as soon as you can after cutting, being careful not to steam the delicate flower heads. Then arrange as normal. However, don't expect too much from them as hellebores are fleeting beauties – two or three days at most.

Spikes & spires

An easy way to add a "garden-grown" feel to an arrangement is to put together flowers with varied shapes – a spike or spire will break out from the main "dome" of your display and add a looser, more natural feel as well as extra height.

DELPHINIUMS (*DELPHINIUM*)

These glorious spires can tower to over 6 ft (1⅘ m), but I generally find the shorter varieties more useful. I've bought delphiniums as potted plants in the past, but to make it affordable to harvest armloads it's best to grow them from seed. Germination is famously erratic, so I pop the seed packet in the freezer for a week. I've found this helps a little.

Delphiniums need full sun with well-drained soil – add small stones or sand if needed. The plants will rot and disappear over winter if they are waterlogged. Watch out for slug damage – these mollusks love the young shoots. Being hungry feeders, delphiniums need a liquid feed a couple of times through the season and a mulch in spring. Cut the plants back to the ground after flowering, to encourage a second flush of flowers in late summer. Pick when most of the flowers are open – they should last about a week from this stage.

Belladonna Group 'Bellamosum' – striking, dark violet-blue flowers. Height 30–35 in (75–90cm).
'Magic Fountains Pure White' – densely packed spires of semi-double, white blooms. Height 30-35 in (75-90cm).
'Centurion White' – magnificent statuesque white blooms with delicate apple green-flushed centers. Height 71 in (180cm).

LUPINS (*LUPINUS*)

A cottage-garden herbaceous perennial that is undemanding in the garden (and the vase). Ideally, it needs well-drained, neutral to acid soil in full sun, but it can take a little shade. If your soil is chalky, don't plant lupins – they'll never thrive. Cut when three-quarters of the flowers are open and sear the stems for 30 seconds in boiling water to extend vase life – they should last about 7 days. By cutting the flowers for the vase you are extending the flowering period and smaller secondary flowers will form from the sideshoots underneath your cut. The varieties available as seeds are numerous and they are easy to propagate and grow on, with some flowering in their first year.

L. **'Noble Maiden'** – soft ivory-white buds that open to pure clean white. Height 35 in (90cm).
L. **'Beefeater'** – stunning red variety with densely packed flower spikes that are long-lasting. Height 35 in (90cm).
L. **'Terracotta'** – beautiful shade of orangy pink. Height 35 in (90cm).
L. **Gallery Series** – comes in pinks, blues and whites. Widely available cheaply as small potted plants in early spring; will establish quickly. Height 24 in (60cm).

GOOSENECK/LOOSESTRIFE
(*LYSIMACHIA CLETHROIDES*)

The delicate arching spires that sit above the dark green leaves of this herbaceous perennial in late summer add a sense of movement to an arrangement. It's pretty and elegant enough to cut just a few stems to have in a small tumbler beside the bed. Gooseneck likes full sun, but will take part shade. Expect around 5–7 days in the vase. Height 35 in (90cm).

BELLFLOWERS (*CAMPANULA PERSICIFOLIA*)

This cottage-garden favorite has tall upright stems (that will need staking or they'll be floored in the rain). My favorite one is *C.p.* var. *alba,* which carries bell-shaped blooms in white. It's great for adding height to an arrangement and is long flowering. Pick when two or three of the flowers are open. They should last 7–10 days in the vase. Height 24 in (60cm).

ABOVE, CLOCKWISE FROM TOP LEFT: An unknown variety of delphinium picked in a friend's garden, *D.* 'Centurion White' is similar; lupin. 'Purple Gallery'; gooseneck; bellflower. OPPOSITE: *D.* 'Magic Fountains Sky Blue'.

Arches & curves

For grace of movement, it's difficult to beat arching stems that can sweep up and out of an arrangement to create a sense of flow. They add an organic feel to a display and help create that loose, wild, sprawling look I'm so fond of.

SOLOMAN'S SEAL (*POLYGONATUM X HYBRIDUM*)

This springtime favorite has graceful, arching stems bearing small tubular flowers that dangle from beneath the leaves from mid-spring to summer. This herbaceous perennial is at home in a woodland setting so a spot with dappled shade is best. Buy these as bare-root plants in autumn or winter to pot and then plant in spring. Expect a vase life of around 7–10 days. Height 39–51 in (100–130cm).

BLEEDING HEART (*LAMPROCAPNOS SPECTABILIS 'ALBA'*)

Another one for a shady cutting garden is this herbaceous perennial, which has heart-shaped flowers that hang from arching stems in spring. It dislikes full sun so a shady position is ideal. It needs good drainage but doesn't like to dry out. Expect a vase life of around 7–10 days. Height 24–35 in (60–90cm).

ABOVE: Solomon's seal.
OPPOSITE: *Lamprocapnos spectabilis* 'Alba'

Little bit of quirk

These plants, which develop tufts, pincushions, and classic daisy shapes, are the ones that will bring a little bit of magic to your arrangements. You may not have a whole vase of them, but a single stem in a little bottle or a few added to an arrangement takes things up a notch and will make your displays unique.

AVENS (*GEUM*)

These herbaceous perennials are often overlooked as a cut flower, but I love the way they add a little something different to an arrangement. Vase life is around 5–7 days.

'Mai Tai' – long, red-tinged stem with pink-flushed, apricot flowers that bloom from midsummer onwards. It's almost frilly and looks semi-double. Height 18 in (45cm).
'Totally Tangerine' – slightly taller variety with bright-orange flowers. Has a particularly long flowering period from late spring to early autumn. Height 24 in (60cm).

JAPANESE ANEMONES (*ANEMONE HUPEHENSIS & A. × HYBRIDA*)

A herbaceous perennial with sophisticated-looking blooms that appeals at every stage from bud to seedhead. They will last around 10 days in the vase.

A. × hybrida 'September Charm' – stunning coloring with stems and pale pink petals tinted on the outside with purple. Height 35 in (90cm).
A. × hybrida 'Honorine Jobert' – beautiful, larger-flowered, white variety. Height 39 in (100cm).
A. hupehensis – taller still, with rose-mauve flowers. Part shade is ideal, where it will spread quite quickly – some may think a little too quickly. Height 47 in (120cm).

GRANNY'S BONNETS (*AQUILEGIA VULGARIS*)

This quintessential cottage-garden herbaceous perennial adds a little point of difference to homegrown bunches from early summer – I rarely see it for sale in florists. I prefer the frilly, tufted, fully double types for the vase, which come in too many beautiful colors to mention. When sown under cover early, they will flower in their first year. Sear the stems in water when conditioning to help extend vase life to around 5 days.

A. vulgaris var. *stellata* 'Ruby Port' – rich burgundy, velvet flowers. Height 35 in (90cm).

A. 'Lime Sorbet' – beautiful, pale limy white. Height 35 in (90cm).

MASTERWORT (*ASTRANTIA*)

A herbaceous perennial that flowers in early summer with pincushion-shaped blooms that have a delicate, ephemeral, papery quality. It's a plant that can tolerate a little bit of shade. Masterwort has a long vase life of around two weeks.

A. major 'Large White' – white flowers on a slightly grander scale that other varieties and tipped with green at the edges of the petals. Height 35 in (90cm).
A. 'Moulin Rouge' – spectacular variety with ruby-red flowers and dark green stems and leaves. Height 24 in (60cm).

OPPOSITE: *Aquilegia* 'Lime Sorbet'.
ABOVE: Astrantia *major* 'Large White'.
TOP RIGHT: Geum ' Mai Tai'.

BOTTOM RIGHT: *Anemone* × *hybrida* 'September Charm'.

Foam & froth

Floral fillers act as a bridge between the secondary flowers and the foliage, they help create balance within an arrangement, filling space and adding more floral interest without taking over from the hero or secondary flowers. They help soften things up and add another textural element.

SEDUMS (*HYLOTELEPHIUM*)

This herbaceous perennial has thick, succulent-like, stout stems topped with flattened flower heads formed of clusters of star-shaped flowers that make the perfect floral filler in late summer and autumn. They are super easy to grow (and propagate as cuttings in summer or autumn) as well as being hardy and have a fantastic vase life. Sedums last for over 2 weeks in the vase and dry well.

'Matrona' – soft pink flowers with leaves flushed with purple and bronze. Height 30 in (75cm).

'Herbstfreude' – a widely grown variety with rich pink flowers. Height 24 in (60cm).

YARROW (*ACHILLEA MILLEFOLIUM*)

Feathery foliage with flat, umbel-shaped flower heads make a fantastic filler. Yarrow is easy to grow if you give it heat and sunshine and will repeat bloom from early summer onwards if you keep picking. It tends to die back at the center of the plant after a couple of seasons, so should be divided every three years or so. Easy to grow from seed and will flower in the first year if sown early.

'Cerise Queen' – vibrant pink flowers. Height 24 in (60cm).

Summer Pastels Group – softer shades of pink, lilac, apricot-peach and purple. Height 24 in (60cm).

RIGHT: *Hylotelephium* 'Herbstfreude'.
ABOVE, RIGHT: Achilliea Millefolium 'Cerise Queen'
OPPOSITE, LEFT: *Phlox paniculata* 'David'
OPPOSITE, RIGHT: Lady's mantle mixed with feverfew, another great filler perennial plant, and zinnias

PERENNIAL PHLOX (*PHLOX PANICULATA*)

Phlox has an old-fashioned charm. Clusters of flowers form a large flower head borne on long stems during high summer and are so useful in arranging, while the bonus is delicious, intense, honey perfume. Colors available include white to red, with nearly every shade of pink, lavender, and purple in between, and there are also bicolored ones. I stick to the classic white of *P. paniculata* 'David' as it seems to go with just about everything – I use it to fill out larger arrangements or become a secondary flower in smaller displays. Give the plants plenty of sun and rich soil, and keep picking and you'll be rewarded with repeat blooms through summer. Harvest when the blooms are just opening for the best vase life of around 5–7 days. Some of the flowers within the cluster will fade during that time, but it's easy to dislodge those with a gentle shake and the smaller buds will open to take their place.

P. paniculata 'David' – vigorous grower with white blooms and some resistance to powdery mildew, which can be a problem for phlox. Height 35–47 in (90–120cm).

LADY'S MANTLE (*ALCHEMILLA MOLLIS*)

Large sprays of chartreuse flowers held above scalloped-edged leaves make this herbaceous perennial a must for me. It's as easy in the garden as it is in the vase – self-seeding rampantly if you don't cut all the flowers. It makes the perfect, lime-green froth to fill out early summer arrangements. Cut back after the first flowering, to encourage a second flowering in late summer or early autumn. Sear the stems in water when conditioning. Expect a vase life of ten days. Height 20 in (50cm).

ABOVE: Lichen-covered apple blossom from my garden.
OPPOSITE: Cherry blossom.

Flowering branches

Flowering branches add a real picked-from-the-garden feel to your arrangements – a few shorter stems nestled in among spring bulbs in a vase will give height and structure, but it's when you scale things up and raid the garden for branches and arrange them en masse that the real magic happens.

CHERRY (*PRUNUS*)

It's hard to beat the beauty of cherry blossom with its frothy, cotton candy clouds of papery pink or white confetti. I don't have a tree in my garden, but I'm given free rein on a friend's each spring, and I love bringing the stems indoors and watching them open – sadly neither of us knows the variety.

'Shirofugen' – clusters of soft blush blooms on long stalks that look stunning against the emerging bronze foliage that turns to green, then orange and red in autumn. Height 26 ft (800cm).

'Royal Burgundy' – deep wine-burgundy leaves of much smaller proportions than 'Shirofugen'. Height 16 ft (500cm).

APPLE (*MALUS*)

We were lucky enough to inherit an old apple tree at the bottom of the garden when we bought our cottage. Its branches are covered in a mustard-colored lichen that makes the stems look like they've been haphazardly flocked in velvet. Its apples taste delicious so I can't bring myself to cut more than a few small branches off the tree for the house and thereby sacrifice all those potential fruits in the process. Instead, when I'm doing the annual winter pruning (always later than planned), I'll have a go at forcing the stems I've had to prune, instead of putting them on the compost heap.

MAGNOLIA (*MAGNOLIA*)

At the house where I grew up, there's an old *M. × soulangeana* that is festooned with beautiful, white, tulip-shaped flowers blushed with soft pinky purple. We've positioned a long table beneath its twisted limbs, which have begun to embrace one corner of the house, and for a couple of weeks in spring we have the joy of sitting beneath its canopy of exquisite, lightly fragranced blooms. Sometimes, a visit to see my dad magically coincides with the magnolia at its peak, but more often than not I'm a little early or late. If I'm there as the buds are just plumping up, I'll snip a branch or two to take back home, to force in a vase (see Fast-Forwarding Spring, right).

One day I'll take a cutting of my dad's tree, but meanwhile there are a few others I have on my horticultural lust-list.

M. stellata – smaller than *M. × soulangeana* and perfect for the back of mixed borders, it can even be grown in pots. It has the most wonderful fragrant, pure white, star-shaped flowers in spring. Height 7 ft (200cm).

M. stellata 'Rosea' – starts out a pretty pale pink before fading to white. The leaves on both can take on bronze tints in summer. Height 7 ft (200cm).

FAST-FORWARDING SPRING

It's possible to cheat the seasons and force flowering branches into bloom earlier by bringing them indoors. The process itself is actually pretty straightforward; the tricky part can be getting the timing of harvesting right. Many trees and shrubs require a period of cold before they bloom. Professional growers get very scientific about making sure they get the timings right, so they can pick at the earliest opportunity, but I just make things easy for myself and try to stay close to the natural flowering time when plants are more likely to bloom – I wait until the buds have started to plump up before I pick them. If you pick too early, the flowers won't be mature enough within the buds and they won't flower.

❊ Cut pencil-thick branches with plump buds; these will be easier to force than thicker branches.

❊ Make sure you have a branch with flower buds, which are slightly fatter than leaf buds. (If you are struggling to tell the difference – chop one in half and you'll see the immature flower parts inside.)

❊ Cut a "V" shape out of the bottom of the stem (pointing upwards), then place the stem base in a bucket with warm water and flower food. Keep the stem in a cool place such as a porch or a garage, where the temperature is 45–50°F (7–10°C) and then arrange once the buds start to color.

❊ The buds and any developing flowers are super delicate, so handle the stems as little as you can and be gentle when you're arranging.

❊ Alternatively, you could arrange the stems straight after picking and put them somewhere prominent – I like to watch the progress as the buds swell and finally burst open. Keep changing the water every couple of days, adding more flower food/preservative each time. If the flowers don't open, it may be that you've cut too early – just try again a little later.

BRANCHES I LIKE TO FORCE:

Flowering quince (*Chaenomeles*)

Pussy willow (*Salix discolor*)

Apple and crab apple (*Malus*)

Cherry (*Prunus*)

Witch hazel (*Hamamelis vernalis*)

Magnolia (*Magnolia*)

Lilac (*Syringa*)

Mock orange (*Philadelpus*)

RIGHT: *Magnolia stellata.*
BELOW: Foraged cherry blossom.

HARVESTING & CONDITIONING

❋ Cut first thing in the morning, bringing a bucket of water out to the garden with you to place the stems in straight away. Use a pair of sharp pruning shears – you want to leave a clean cut on the tree, to prevent damage.

❋ The stems are woody, so you'll need to condition them by cutting a "V" shape pointing upwards from the bottom of each stem, with a sharp knife or some shears. Then place each stem in warm water with flower food/preservative for a few hours, before arranging. (For more conditioning tips, see pages 226–229).

ABOVE: Apple blossom.
LEFT AND OPPOSITE: *Magnolia* x *soulangeana*.

Flowering shrubs

If you have space in your garden for a couple more shrubs, it's worthwhile considering one that also makes a great cut flower – once they've grown to a decent size, you'll be able to harvest generous amounts for the house without sacrificing too much of their beauty in the garden. Although they are an investment initially, they are incredibly low, almost no, maintenance and will get bigger and better year after year. Flowering shrubs create a real point of difference to your flowers and add substance and mass to your arrangements.

COMMON LILAC (*SYRINGA VULGARIS*)

It took me a while to get over the old wives' tale of it being bad luck to bring lilac into the house, but when we moved to our cottage and inherited an old purple lilac I couldn't resist picking bucket-loads for indoors. Admittedly, lilacs have a short flowering season, but the beauty and knockout fragrance of their blue, pink, white, or, of course, lilac blooms more than make up for it in my mind. The varieties below are all deciduous with heart-shaped leaves and dense pannicles of highly scented flowers.

'Madame Lemoine' – a stunning white double with a fantastic vase life of over a week. Height 13 ft (400cm).

'Charles Joly' – has densely packed magenta, double flowers. Height 16 ft (500cm).

'Katherine Havemeyer' – has pretty lavender-purple double flowers that fade to lilac-pink flowers. Height 23 ft (700cm).

IN THE GARDEN

Lilacs are low maintenance – give them good soil, full sun, and a mulch of organic matter in the spring and they will reward you with plenty of blooms. You won't need to do much pruning if you are cutting for flowers. Once the lilac becomes established, if you're not harvesting all the blooms, cut some of the taller branches back immediately after flowering in mid-summer to encourage flowers on lower branches. Lilacs flower on old wood so the timing of this pruning is important or you won't have flowers the following year.

IN THE VASE

Harvest when about a third of the flowers have opened. They do have a tendency to wilt, so to help prevent this, condition properly with warm water and flower food and keep somewhere cold and dark, if possible overnight.

ABOVE: A bucket of foraged lilac.
OPPOSITE: Deep purple 'Charles Joly' and white 'Madame Lemonie' with foraged lilac.

ABOVE: Philadelphus
(Mock Orange)
ABOVE LEFT: Viburnum Opulus
'Roseum' (Snowball bush)
OPPOSITE: *Pieris japonica* with
hellebores, tulips, and catkins

SNOWBALL BUSH (*VIBURNUM OPULUS* 'ROSEUM')

This has to be my favorite spring-flowering shrub. It's absolutely covered in small pom-poms that start out a bright acidic green, softening to creamy green and then finish as pure white. This deciduous shrub, which is tolerant of most soils, has maple-like leaves that become purple-tinted in autumn, so it's invaluable as foliage later in the season. It can take some shade, too, which is a bonus: I have three of these in a north-west-facing border and they are flourishing. They will reach 13 ft (4m) when mature (and the same in spread), but I'm not sure mine will ever get the chance as I cut them so much. The stems need searing for 45 seconds when conditioning, but will then last for around two weeks in a vase. Otherwise, treat as any other woody cut. Height 13 ft (400cm).

MOCK ORANGE (*PHILADELPHUS*)

This plant is sometimes considered to be old-fashioned in garden planting schemes, but as a cut flower mock orange is magnificent and well worth the space if you have it. This deciduous shrub likes most soils and is smothered with pure white flowers in late spring and early summer, which are highly fragranced with a scent said to resemble orange blossom – hence the common name "mock orange." Harvest when the flower buds are just opening. Expect a vase life of 5–10 days. I pick from

an unknown single variety in my dad's garden.

'Virginal' – large, double-flowered with exceptional scent and delicate-looking, pure white blooms. Height 10 ft (300cm).

'Belle Étoile' – another plant that's on my wishlist. it has large single white blooms flushed with purple at their centers. Height 5 ft (150cm).

LILY OF THE VALLEY SHRUB (*PIERIS JAPONICA*)

This evergreen shrub makes a fabulous floral filler, with its chains of urn-shaped blooms that open in spring. It has a wonderful texture and adds a sense of movement to arrangements as the showy flower clusters arch and lean over the edge of the vase. It is an acid-lover, but you can grow the compact varieties in pots if your soil is too alkaline. The flowers are long-lasting in the vase – expect around seven days.

'White Cascade' – white flowers. Height 10 ft (300cm).
japonica 'Purity' – compact and bears white flowers. Height 3–5 ft (100–150cm).

Flowering climbers

For sheer abundance of blooms, you can't beat a flowering climber. Plant one in your garden and let its twining stems ramble their way up and over a wall, tree, or trellis, giving you generous cutting material for many years to come. These flowering trails – rarely available as cut flowers – will give your arrangements a romantic, wild feel.

CLEMATIS (*CLEMATIS*)

It's easy to assume that the thin wiry stems of clematis won't hold up in a arrangement, but its vase life can be exceptionally good – you just need to choose the right varieties and sear the stems when conditioning. In recent years, breeders have developed Amazing Series especially for cutting. I have yet to try these in my garden, but after seeing them at the RHS Chelsea Flower Show, they've made it onto my wishlist. Each is named after a city; I particularly like 'Amazing London'.

In terms of other clematis that make suitable cut flowers, in general, consider ones from the Viticella, Texensis, and Integrifolia Groups as they are prolific enough for cutting as well as lasting in the vase. These Groups particularly appeal to me as their pruning regime is so easy: it's just one hard cut back to nearly ground level in late winter. The Tangutica Group is also worth looking at as it produces decorative seedheads that are perfect for arranging in winter.

Clematis are tolerant of most soils, but like a sunny spot with their roots shaded. They may need a little help to get started climbing, but will make their own way soon enough.

'**Amazing London**' – large, pale lilac flowers with a vase life of more than two weeks. Height 5–7 ft (150cm–200cm).

C. **Princess Kate (Texensis Group)** – lily-shaped, white flowers with dark pink shading on the outside of the petals. Easy to prune. Height 8–11 ft (250–350cm)

C. montana var. *rubens* – sweetly scented, pale-pink flowers in early summer. It's a vigorous variety. Lovely green foliage tinged with bronze is useful for picking to use as trails. No pruning required, just tidy after flowering when needed. Height 23 ft (700cm).

'**Bill MacKenzie**' – stunning, yellow, nodding flowers with the texture of lemon peel, which flower in early and midsummer, then puffball seedheads follow. Height 10–13 ft (300–400cm).

HONEYSUCKLE (*LONICERA*)

This summer-flowering climber has such an exquisite, spicy-sweet perfume when in full bloom that it often stops me in my tracks when I'm out and about. It's a tough plant that will thrive in most soils and can take a bit of shade, but you will get more flowers in a sunny spot. Vase life for honeysuckle isn't long – just a few days, but the scent more than makes up for it. Searing the stems will help.

L. periclymenum '**Graham Thomas**' – deciduous, vigorous and fast-growing with soft-yellow flowers. Height 23 ft (700cm).

L. periclymenum '**Rhubarb and Custard**' – a more compact, deciduous form with pretty pink-purple flowers and a long flowering period. Height 7 ft (200cm).

OPPOSITE, CLOCKWISE FROM TOP LEFT: *Clematis montana* as filler among tulips and fritillaria in a spring arrangement; *C.* 'Princess Kate'; *Lonicera periclymenum* 'Graham Thomas'; *C. Montana* 'Rubens'; 'Bill Mackenzie' *clematis montana* var. *rubens*.

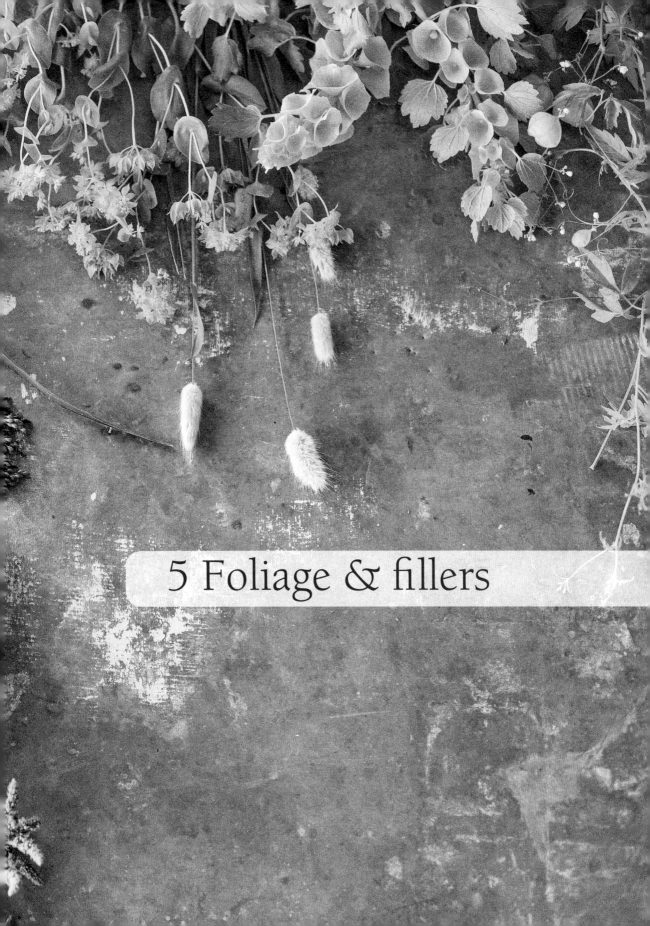

5 Foliage & fillers

The backbone of your mixed arrangements

Don't make the mistake I did in thinking that flower arranging is all about the flowers – it's not. In the same way a landscape designer might think of trees and shrubs as the "bones" of a planting scheme, your foliage and fillers will provide you with the backbone to your arrangements – a foil to offset your blooms.

IN THE GARDEN

❀ Your garden may already be a rich source of foliage and fillers. If there's anything that you like the look of, cut and try some inside, to test for vase life. Some foliage doesn't last at all when cut and can wilt literally before your eyes – especially the first flush of spring growth.

❀ One of the joys of growing your own is that you can control when you harvest your crop – you decide if you want to pick a flower in bud or full bloom, or whether to leave foliage to take on an autumn hue or deliberately let plants go to seed so that you can harvest the interesting seed pods to add texture to your displays. Be open to experimenting and trying new things – not only in the vase but in the garden.

IN THE VASE

❀ It's helpful to think of foliage in terms of how you're going to use it. The "structural" foliage comprises the sturdier woody branches that dictate the scale and shape of your arrangement, while the "soft" foliage is used to pad out and fill your arrangements. Structural foliage is normally the first thing I'll add to a vase when I'm building a mixed arrangement, followed by any soft foliage.

❀ A filler is something that you might not put in a vase and enjoy by itself, but is invaluable for arranging, filling in any awkward gaps, and adding texture and a sense of airiness and movement to floral displays.

❀ Just as you think carefully about your flowers in terms of choice of color, form, texture, etc., the same should be true of your foliage and fillers. Your choice will alter the feel, look, and style of an arrangement. Use them as an opportunity to add another layer of interest – a bunch of scented leaves, strokable fluffy grass, a cluster of bead-like, glossy seedheads, or a branch of tree foliage with leaves in a myriad of autumnal hues will all make your displays unique and take them to another level.

❀ "Greenery" doesn't have to be "green" – the color options open to you are endless. In my garden I use the brooding plums and burgundies of copper beech, ninebark, and coral bells alongside the blue-green of lush annual honeywort and the soft gray/silver of furry textured dusty miller. Foliage is an equal to your flowers in terms of bringing color to your displays.

LEFT: A bucket of mixed foliage from the cutting garden.
OPPOSITE, TOP: Dahlias with green-topped sage and mixed grasses.
OPPOSITE, RIGHT: Mixed grasses growing beside amaranthus and zinnias.

Foliage annuals

These are the powerhouses of my cutting garden, providing most of the foliage and filler material to bulk out my arrangements. They are all must-haves because of their form, color, and texture.

HONEYWORT (*CERINTHE MAJOR* 'PURPURASCENS')

Such a beautiful and satisfyingly fleshy foliage plant with shades of purple, silver, and green on the same plant. It has the added bonus of delicate, nodding, bell-shaped flowers adored by bees. It's a great hardy annual for a direct autumn sowing, to give you early foliage in spring. I then sow again in spring for a later crop. I pick bucket-loads of this – it's probably my number-one foliage plant. When conditioning, sear the ends of spring-harvested stems to prevent them from drooping. Vase life is excellent at 7–10 days. Height 24 in (60cm).

BELLS OF IRELAND (*MOLUCCELLA LAEVIS*)

These tall green spires with bell-shaped blooms (technically, calyces that encase the actual tiny white blooms) are striking enough to take center stage in a vase by themselves, but are a great way to bring height to an arrangement as well as add plenty of substance.

They also dry well. Bells of Ireland is a half-hardy annual and a little slow to get going, so I start my seeds off under cover about two months before the last frosts are anticipated. Germination can be a little tricky, but I've found putting the seeds in the freezer for a week before sowing helps germination rates. If you want to showcase the "bells" more, strip off some of the leaves around the blooms. Watch out when handling the stems as they are quite prickly. Vase life is 7–10 days. Height 35 in (90cm).

BORAGE (*BORAGO OFFICINALIS*)

Borage is often overlooked as a cut flower as its star-shaped blooms are tiny, but I find both the blue and white varieties very useful to bulk out arrangements and add a little element of wildness to proceedings. I sow two batches of seeds direct: one in autumn and one in spring. The stems have fine little prickles on them so take care when handling. Borage can be a bit of a brute and is a

LEFT: *Salvia viridis* 'Blue' and 'Pink'.
OPPOSITE AND ABOVE, LEFT TO RIGHT: Honeywort; bells of Ireland; white borage and hare's ear.

prolific self-seeder when the conditions are right, so keep cutting if you don't want masses of babies everywhere. Expect a vase life of around seven days. Height 35 in (90cm).

GREEN-TOPPED SAGE (*SALVIA VIRIDIS* 'BLUE' & 'PINK')

It may not have been love at first sight, but these hardy annuals are such a steady performer in the garden and provide masses of filler to pick from early summer to autumn that they now make it onto my growing list each year. I start mine off under cover four weeks before the last frosts, but they can be direct sown in autumn and spring. The "flowers" are, in fact, colorful veined bracts, which not only have a good vase life – averaging around ten days – but dry well, too. Try *S. viridis* 'White Swan' for white bracts. Height 18 in (45cm).

HARE'S EAR (*BUPLEURUM ROTUNDIFOLIUM* 'GARIBALDI')

Delicate, bright green flowers and foliage keeps going for two to three months. The secret to success that I have learned after a few failed attempts is to direct sow the seeds. They need light to germinate, so don't cover them with soil. Be sure to pre-water the soil so you don't wash away the seeds. I do two sowings: one in autumn for harvesting in spring; and a second in spring for a summer harvest. Vase life is about ten days. Height 35 in (90cm).

ABOVE, LEFT: Red-leaf Hibiscus with carnations, sedum, and dusty miller in a late summer posy.
ABOVE: Basil 'Aromatto'.
OPPOSITE: Dusty miller 'New Look' with 'Harry Edland' roses, wild carrot 'Purple Kisses', and basil 'Aromatto'.

DUSTY MILLER (*SENECIO CINERARIA* 'NEW LOOK')

It's the tactile, immensely strokable, furry texture of these silvery-gray leaves that make this plant so appealing. It's technically a tender perennial, but grown as an annual. Sow seeds 8–10 weeks before the last frost is anticipated and plant out when all risk of frost has gone. It is started off early as the stems need to harden up a bit before they can be cut, otherwise they'll wilt. Put them into water straight away after cutting and condition well. They should last 7–10 days. Height 2 in (30cm).

BASIL (*OCIMUM BASILICUM* 'AROMATTO')

This is a recent addition to my cutting garden and one that I'm loving as it's so rarely seen in bouquets in the shops. As well as the deep plum-purple, aromatic leaves, you get the bonus of the flower spikes. Start the half-hardy annual seeds off under cover about six weeks before the last frost. Then wait until well after the last frosts before you plant out – as with all basils. 'Aromatto' is very sensitive to the cold. It tends to wilt when picked too soon, so wait for the stems to harden up (or the flower spikes to form). It should then last around seven days in the vase. Height 24 in (60cm).

RED-LEAF HIBISCUS (*HIBISCUS* 'MAHOGANY SPLENDOR')

Although technically a perennial, this plant is grown as a half-hardy annual. I sow mine 4–6 weeks before the last frost. It has the most wonderful, rich burgundy, maple-shaped leaves with serrated edges. The leaves darken as they mature during the season. Stems last in the vase for around seven days. Height 35 in (90cm).

Foliage perennials & shrubs

Perhaps not the first choice for a cutting garden, but once established, they will supply you with plenty of leafy material through the year. I tend to steer clear of the classic types of "greenery" commonly available in florist shops and instead opt for plants with unusual form or color.

NINEBARK (*PHYSOCARPUS OPULIFOLIUS* 'DIABOLO')

This hardy deciduous shrub is best in full sun, but tolerates part shade. Its beautiful purple-coppery bronze, maple-like foliage starts out bronze-green when young and is ready to harvest from midsummer. Earlier in the season it tends to droop when growth is new and soft. In midsummer, pink-tinged, white flowers appear, which form red seed clusters in autumn. Vase life is excellent – expect around ten days. Height 79 in (200cm).

CORAL BELLS (*HEUCHERA*)

These herbaceous perennials may not be an obvious choice – I began using them after visiting the garden of flower grower and florist Susanne Hatwood of The Blue Carrot in Cornwall. The wispy-stemmed, bell-shaped flowers are a lovely bonus, but it's the foliage that's the star. It comes in some amazing colors, from burgundy, ruby and bronze to silver, burnt ocher and acidic yellow (as well as green). Many have interesting mottling or marbling, with ruffled or lobed leaves that can be textured, too. They are best in part shade, where their leaves won't fade or be scorched by sun. Choose a variety that works best for your color palette,

but pay attention to the heights– some are quite short. Expect a vase life of around ten days.

'Caramel' has unusual, honey-apricot leaves that unfurl as bright gold with cream flowers in summer; a useful contrast for dusky pinks and blush colors. Height 20 in (50cm).

H. villosa 'Palace Purple' has deep purple leaves with an almost metallic look. Height 24 in (60cm).

DAISY BUSH (*BRACHYGLOTTIS* DUNEDIN GROUP)

I saw this evergreen shrub in a neighbor's garden and fell in love with the texture of the leaves. The undersides are heavily felted, making them a beautiful silvery white, while the uppersides of the leaves remain a soft gray-green with younger growth appearing lighter in color. The plant has masses of daisy-like, bright yellow flowers in summer, which don't do a thing for me. With regular harvesting, the flowers never have a chance to bloom and I'm rewarded with more of the soft silvery new growth. It likes a sunny spot. Vase life is very good – expect around ten days. Height 47 in (120cm).

OPPOSITE, FAR LEFT: *Heuchera* 'Caramel'.
OPPOSITE, LEFT: A work in progress – Ninebark, coral bells, and copper beech foliage form the basic structure for a bowl arrangement before blooms are added.

ABOVE: *Brachyglottis* 'Sunshine'.
LEFT: *Physocarpus opulifolius* 'Diabolo'.

Scented foliage, herbs & aromatics

Whenever I add a sprig of something fragrant in a bouquet, it's one of the first things people comment on as they bring the bunch up to their nose to take in the scent. Using aromatic foliage adds another layer of fragrance to your blooms and a real sense of vibrancy and freshness.

SCENTED GERANIUMS (*PELARGONIUM* 'ATTAR OF ROSES')

Another absolute must-have for me in the cutting garden is *P.* 'Attar of Roses'. Its rose scent from the leaves is incredible and elevates a simple posy into something extraordinary.

Scented geraniums are tender perennials and will be damaged by frost, so you'll need to think about what you'll do with them over winter. I grow mine grouped together in giant pots outdoors with lots of grit in full sun and overwinter them in the greenhouse (repotting them individually into smaller pots). They'll spend winter in a semi-dormant state. If you don't have a greenhouse, anywhere that's just frost-free and bright will do – a porch or a windowsill in an unheated room will work. Keep plants on the moist side of dry. In late winter, they'll start to wake up as the light levels increase. That's when I give them a good pruning to stop them going leggy, a top dressing of new soil (or a bigger pot if needed), and a liquid feed to start them off well for the new season. Vase life is exceptional: they last for up to three weeks in the vase – often producing roots. Height 18 in (45cm).

HOW TO TAKE CUTTINGS OF SCENTED GERANIUMS

As they're one of the easiest plants to propagate, it's immensely satisfying being able to increase your stock for free. I take cuttings in early autumn (to overwinter) and in spring.

❋ Fill a small square pot with well-drained compost – I use 50:50 multipurpose potting compost and perlite or vermiculite – and firm down gently.

❋ Choose a stem with no flowers, then cut just above a leaf node with pruning shears.

❋ Using a sharp knife, remove the lower leaves and cut the bottom of the stem straight across just below a leaf node.

❋ Make a hole in the compost with a pencil and put your cutting in. Give it a good watering and then pop it somewhere well-lit but out of direct sunlight, such as a windowsill or an unheated greenhouse. Ideally, it should have a bit of bottom heat, to speed things up.

❋ Cuttings shouldn't need too much watering, but make sure they don't dry out. They normally take around eight weeks to root, after which they'll be ready to plant and grow.

OPPOSITE, CLOCKWISE FROM TOP: A mixed late-summer posy of roses, mint, and bishop's flower with grasses; *Pelargonium* 'Attar of Roses' growing in large pots in the cutting garden; rooted cuttings about to be potted individually.

ABOVE, FROM LEFT TO RIGHT: Apple
mint, chocolate mint, spearmint
OPPOSITE, LEFT: I have dedicated a
raised bed to mint in the vegetable
patch. OPPOSITE, RIGHT: Apple mint..
OPPOSITE, BOTTOM: A wreath made.
from sprigs of rosemary.

MINT (*MENTHA*)

One of the most useful foliage plants in my cutting garden, mint has the bonus of prettily spiked flowers. I keep picking and picking all season long as mint goes with absolutely everything. Lots of people are a little scared to plant this herbaceous perennial in their garden as it has a reputation for being a bit thuggish and spreading like wildfire. I love it so much that I've dedicated a whole raised bed to it – so it's confined within that 4 × 6½ ft (1⅕ × 2m) space. I recommend you do the same. Alternatively, bury a large pot in the ground and plant into that; leave the rim slightly above the soil level, to curb its quest for world domination. I always tend to buy plants (small 3.5 in [9cm] pots) or take root cuttings rather than sow from seed, as mint bulks up so quickly. It's a low-maintenance plant, thrives in poor soil and can even take a little shade, but it does need dividing every few years and in dry weather a good watering will do it the world of good.

Try not to harvest the stems in the heat of the day as they do have a tendency to wilt, especially when in flower. Mint has a long vase life of a 7–10 days and is always the last one standing in a mixed bouquet.

Apple mint (*M. suaveolens*) – large, soft, gray-green, furry leaves with spikes of pink flowers in late summer. This is the one I always go to first, pruning shears in hand, as I love the softness it brings to a bouquet. Height 35 in (90cm).

Chocolate mint (*Mentha* x *piperita f. citrata* 'Chocolate') – another one of my favorites, with its dark brown stems and chocolate coloring to the leaves. Height 20–39 in (50–100cm).

Spearmint (*M. spicata*) I grow this mainly for mint tea, but it always ends up in my arrangements as it's so prolific. It's a lovely vivid green with a magnificent scent. Height 39 in (100cm).

ROSEMARY (*ROSMARINUS*)

As an evergreen shrub, rosemary is particularly useful to have in the cutting garden in winter. I think I'd still grow it even if its needle-like leaves didn't give off that beautiful aromatic scent. It is quite slow growing and takes a while to get to the stage where you'll have masses to harvest. While you wait, just use one or two stems in a posy for scent – they will last 7–10 days in a vase. I also make up mini wreaths by attaching small sprigs of rosemary to a circle of heavy-gauge wire, using thin wire to secure them in place. Height 59 in (150cm).

Evergreen climbers

You might not think to plant an evergreen climber as part of your cutting garden, but it makes great fallback material to cut when there's little else available, providing you with greenery and trailing stems to cascade and flow from your arrangements. I'll often weave a few stems through candlesticks dotted down the middle of a dining table as the starting point to form a quick and easy centerpiece.

IVY (*HEDERA HELIX*)

This evergreen, self-clinging shrub, which makes its way up trees and walls, is the one to plant where nothing else will grow in deep shade. It can become invasive so be careful, although if you are cutting regularly it should never become a problem. The lobed leaves we're all familiar with are actually juvenile foliage; the adult flowering stems have oval leaves. I use the younger stems for garlands and the more mature stems as filler foliage. The yellow-green flowers so beloved of bees are followed by clusters of black berries in winter, but they are just as attractive picked in autumn, when the seedheads are vivid green and just plumping up. It lasts for ages in the vase – expect around 10–14 days. Height 33 ft (10m).

JASMINE (*JASMINUM POLYANTHUM*)

Normally sold as a houseplant, I grow jasmine in my greenhouse where it's kept frost-free over winter in bright but not direct sunlight. If you don't have a greenhouse, you could grow it indoors as a houseplant. The heavily scented, star-shaped flowers, which appear in late winter and early spring, are a delight, but it's the fine, graceful, twining foliage that I really grow this jasmine for – it's perfect for winter when there's little else as delicate-looking to do the job. It needs help climbing, but I let it grow free, flowing from the pot. As I cut from it so often, it never has the chance to get out of hand. Vase life is good – around 5–7 days. Height 10 ft (300cm).

OPPOSITE: A "cheat's garland" made by placing flowing branches of copper beech, clusters of mature stems of ivy with berries and a few trails of jasmine down the middle of a table.

ABOVE: Ivy flowing over a neighbor's wall.
LEFT: Frost-tender jasmine in the greenhouse.

Trees

Now I'm not suggesting that you go out and plant any one of these trees as part of your cutting garden (although if you have the space, then why not?). It's more to encourage you to see your existing garden and the plants around you as a florist would – where anything is fair game. Foliage from an established tree gives an arrangement depth and substance. Having the confidence to go out and raid the garden and drag back a 5 ft (1½m) branch for a big-scale arrangement takes your creations into a whole other world.

ABOVE: Oak.
LEFT: Foraged branches of apple mixed with 'Nicholas' dahlias and 'Wollerton Old Hall' roses. OPPOSITE, CLOCKWISE FROM TOP LEFT: Weeping birch; copper beech; hawthorn and Hornbeam

OAK (*QUERCUS*)

The oak has three seasons of interest that make me reach for my pruning shears. There's the lush, vibrant green leaves of spring, then the branches are adorned with clusters of acorns and, finally, it develops the gold- to copper-toned foliage of autumn. This noble tree offers so much and the branches are so beautiful that I'll often arrange them just on their own. Expect a vase life of about seven days. Height 66–148 ft (20–45m).

HORNBEAM (*CARPINUS BETULUS*)

The emerging, bright green leaves are a welcome sight in early spring, when cutting garden foliage can be a little scarce. They provide the archetypal "spring green" to arrangements before their acidic tones mellow to a rich grass green; this turns golden and burnt-orange in autumn. Height 98 ft (30m).

COPPER BEECH (*FAGUS SYLVATICA* ATROPURPUREA GROUP)

Without being lucky enough to inherit the mature copper beech in our garden, I may never have discovered its beauty in the vase. The rich coppery burgundy foliage seems to go with just about everything and has the added interest of textured nut cases in late summer. In autumn, the foliage takes on rich hues of rust and orange. Height 131 ft (40m).

WEEPING BIRCH (*BETULA PENDULA*)

Its pendulous stems are a graceful addition to a vase even when not in leaf. In autumn, the green leaves turn a rich mustard-yellow and are useful to mix with the last of the dahlias, to add a touch of wildness and seasonality to an arrangement. Height 98 ft (30m).

HAWTHORN (*CRATAEGUS MONOGYNA*)

A native hedge borders one side of our garden and keeps me in long-length foliage cuts of hawthorn from spring right through autumn. There's a delightful froth of blossom in spring and then pea-sized, red berries in autumn. Watch for the thorns – they are quite vicious. Height 49 ft (15m).

A WORD ON CONDITIONING
When conditioning, these "woody" cuts prefer warm water. To allow as much water to be soaked up as possible, you'll need to make an upside-down "V" cut into the bottom of the stem (page 229).

LEFT: A little goes a long way –
a few stems of mixed grasses
and cosmos popped into bottles
to decorate the length of a
dining table.
BELOW: *Panicum* 'Frosted Explosion'
adds texture to an arrangement
of roses.
OPPOSITE TOP: Foxtail barley
growing among salvia and scabious.
OPPOSITE BOTTOM: A bed of mixed
grasses, zinnias, and amaranthus.

Grasses

Grasses bring texture to an arrangement, adding softness and a sense of movement. They'll often bob about in the vase as you walk by or if a gentle breeze catches them. I find them so useful, filling in any negative space that I'm left with, the floral equivalent of easing an awkward silence. Grasses also look great when dried – I like to mix them with fresh flowers from late summer onwards.

MY FAVORITES

Violet millet (*Panicum miliaceum* 'Violaceum') –clusters of purple-green, bead-like seedheads that arch over and dangle elegantly. Height 24 in (60cm).

Panicum 'Frosted Explosion' – ethereal puffs of tiny seedheads make a fantastic filler – an absolute must-have every year for me. As the stems age, the explosions gets bigger. Height 16 in (40cm).

Feathertop (*Pennisetum villosum*) – large, creamy white, fluffy spikes. Although technically a perennial, I grow it as an annual as it is tender and won't make it through a bad winter (it's hardy down to 23ºF [-5ºC]). Feathertop can take a little shade. Harvest before the pollen sheds. Height 24 in (60cm).

Fountain grass 'Rubrum' (*Pennisetum* x *advena* 'Rubrum') – soft red-purple spikes with a gentle arching habit. Often grown as an annual as it's only hardy down to 23ºF (-5ºC). Height 59 in (150cm).

Northern sea oats (*Chasmanthium latifolium*) –probably my favorite of all the grasses as it adds a real magic to an arrangement. The flat, heart-shaped flowers that appear on top of wispy stems flutter in any slight breeze. This perennial can take a little shade. Height 24 in (60cm).

Plains bristle grass *(Setaria macrostachya)* – perennial, usually grown as an annual. It has a lovely fuzzy texture, and I love the way it arches and bends over as the flower matures, becoming almost tassle-like. A lovely millet-like ornamental to add arches and curves to your arrangements. Height 32 in (80cm).

Hare's tail (*Lagurus ovatus*) – soft, strokable, fluffy, off-white heads with beautiful, soft gray-green stems and blades. Height 20 in (50cm).

Foxtail barley *(Hordeum jubatum)* – stunning arched spikes of green-gray fluff tinged with purple-red. Height 24 in (60cm).

Black millet *(Sorghum nigrum)* – the giant in my mixed grasses patch. I prefer it when it dries and turns a purple-black. Height 79 in (200cm).

IN THE GARDEN

Grasses are super easy – liking well-drained soil and a sunny spot. It's possible to direct sow in spring, but I start seeds under cover six weeks before the last frost, planting out once there is little risk of frost. I grow most of my grasses from a single packet of mixed seed each spring – I quite like not knowing exactly what might spring up where.

You can harvest most grasses at almost any stage, but the ultra-fluffy ones such as hare's tail or feathertop are best gathered just as the heads have emerged and before the pollen starts to shed.

IN THE VASE

Vase life is good – expect 7–10 days, depending on the variety. Almost all grasses look fantastic dried and it's so simple to do (page 229).

FROM LEFT TO RIGHT: *Panicum* 'Frosted Explosion' and hare's tail; Plains bristle grass; and feathertop; black millet; violet millet and fountain grass 'Rubrum'; northern sea oats.

TOP LEFT: *Atriplex hortensis* 'Green Plume'.
TOP RIGHT: Love-in-a-puff with sweet peas and scabious.
ABOVE: *A. caudatus* 'Viridis'.
LEFT: *A. caudatus*.
OPPOSITE: *Dolichos lablab* 'Ruby Moon'.

Seed pods

Using something from the garden that is unexpected or unusual helps create a little bit of magic in your displays. Stems laden with glossy seed pods, rope-like tassels longer than your arm, or a scattering of papery lanterns are out of the ordinary and an opportunity for you to add another textural element and movement to arrangements.

GARDEN ORACH (*ATRIPLEX HORTENSIS*)

This hardy annual is often overlooked for the cutting patch, but it is popular in the vegetable patch as an alternative to spinach as the young stems and leaves are a delicacy. Let it go to seed before using, to give you clusters of bead-like textural seed pods to fill in arrangements. Three colors are commonly available – the rich reds of 'Red Plume' and 'Copper Plume' and fresh green of 'Green Plume' – often as a mix of all three in one packet. Sear the stems when conditioning and they should last 10–14 days in the vase. Height 59 in (150cm).

HYACINTH BEAN (*DOLICHOS LABLAB* 'RUBY MOON')

This half-hardy annual climber has an almost other-worldly look to it. The bean-like, bicolored, rose-lilac flowers on deep purple stems are pretty in themselves, but it's the seed pods that are the most eye-catching – they resemble varnished, glossy, purple mangetout. Hyacinth bean is a good choice for adding a little bit of eccentricity to your displays. Start seeds under cover in early spring and plant out after the last frosts. Give this climber some support. Expect a vase life of 7–10 days. Height to 10 ft (300cm).

LOVE-IN-A-PUFF (*CARDIOSPERMUM HALICACABUM*)

A half-hardy climbing annual grown for its papery, lantern-like seed pods that form along the ferny-leaved vines. It is a pretty addition to weave into arrangements from summer onwards. I start the seed indoors in early spring and plant outdoors after the frosts. It needs support to climb. Expect around seven days in the vase. Height 10 ft (300cm).

LOVE-LIES-BLEEDING (*AMARANTHUS CAUDATUS*)

A half-hardy annual with stunning, hanging, rich burgundy tassels. Every year, this plant still wows me with its incredible growth. The stems can become quite thick and the tassels heavy, so they need support. I find this plant is better suited to large displays – choose your vase carefully as the tassels can cause a lightweight vase to topple over. I start seed under cover in early spring, but you can also sow direct after the last frosts. 'Viridis' has vivid green tassels, and 'Coral Fountain' has beautiful dusky coral-pink tassels. Expect a vase life of 7–10 days. Height 43 in (110cm).

Catkins

With the leaves on the trees yet to unfurl, these long velvety tassels that drip from the branches of trees and shrubs in late winter and early spring are readily apparent, as if someone has festooned the winter landscape to celebrate the imminent arrival of spring. Catkins are a great way to add scale and texture to an arrangement when there's very little else of interest in the way of branches.

MY FAVORITES

Hazel *(Corylus avellana)* – golden catkins on bare twigs. Height 39 ft (12m).

Silk tassel bush *(Garrya elliptica)* – extra-long catkins, to 10 in (25cm), that are a beautiful velvety gray-green tinged with pink. Height 8–16 ft (200–500cm).

Willow *(Salix gracilistyla* 'Melanostachys'*)* – stunning form of willow with black catkins on red stems. Height 10 ft (300cm).

Alder *(Alnus)* – yellow catkins. Height 82 ft (25m).

HARVESTING

When harvesting branches just as the catkins are beginning to bloom, expect about a week's vase life from this stage. The catkins are male flowers, and their sole purpose is to shed pollen to be taken far and wide in the wind. Bear that in mind when you bring them indoors as they can leave a fine dusting of pollen – enough to turn a table yellow.

ABOVE: Branches of hazel and silk
tassel bush catkins with foraged
evergreen stems of viburnum,
Ligustrum sinense 'Variegatum',
and ivy.

Berries, hips & edible fruits

To bring an air of seasonality to your bunches and a truly "garden-gathered" feel to your displays, add stems of berries, arches of hips, and branches of edible fruits. They make fantastic fillers as well as adding another layer of color and texture.

HIPS

I grow most of my roses for their flowers, to cut and bring into the house. Any that do manage to escape my flower snips are deadheaded, to encourage another flush and so extend the flowering season. Consequently, I rarely get to harvest the fruit, or hips, of the roses in my garden. I therefore forage for them, instead. If you are keen to plant a rose specifically for its hips, most ramblers or climbing roses are suitable as their trusses of flowers become hundreds of hips.

Rosa 'Rambling Rector' – the small, rounded, red hips that are produced in abundance are just a noteworthy as the clouds of semi-double blooms that precede them. Vase life is five days. Height 25 ft (750cm).

Rosa rugosa – large, single, fuchsia-pink flowers followed by exceptionally large, orange hips. Vase life is five days. Height 7 ft (210cm).

Rosa macrophylla 'Master Hugh' – large pink flowers, but it's the large red hips that caught my eye – they hang down like miniature lanterns. Vase life five days. Height 10 ft (300cm).

BERRIES

Nature's little jewels, berries vary enormously in color and size – they all make fantastic fillers. Hedgerows and gardens are full of clusters of pendulous beauties in autumn: for example, hawthorn, whitebeam, and cotoneaster. Pretty much anything is fair game, but watch out as some berries are poisonous. If you are looking for garden varieties and have the space, there are some particularly useful shrubs with berries for arranging.

Snowberry *(Symphoricarpos albus)* – deciduous shrub with arching stems with a profusion of waxy white berries in early autumn. Vase life is 5–7 days. Height 10 ft (300cm).

Symphoricarpos × *doorenbosii* 'Mother of Pearl' – very pretty, pink-flushed berries. Vase life is 5-7 days. Height 10 ft (300cm).

Viburnum tinus – useful evergreen foliage plant to have in the garden in winter, with the bonus of flattened clusters of white flowers from mid-winter to early spring, followed by beautiful, bead-like, blue-black berries with a metallic sheen. Expect a vase life of around ten days. Height 10 ft (300cm).

Beauty berry *(Callicarpa bodinieri* var. *giraldii* 'Profusion')* – beautiful deciduous shrub with small pink flowers in midsummer, while its violet berries appear in autumn. Vase life is 10–14 days. Height 10 ft (300cm).

EDIBLE FRUITS

Think differently about what makes the vase – I'll often raid the vegetable beds for fillers such as a vine of green tomatoes that won't get a chance to ripen at the end of summer, or I'll sacrifice a small branch of apple or damson for a special arrangement as the fruit is starting to plump up. Such items can be just as beautiful as flowers and add the unexpected.

Raspberries *(Rubus idaeus)* and foraged wild blackberries (*R. fruicosus*) – pick just before the fruit ripens so it stays on its stem and is pretty enough to warrant sacrificing the tasty berries. Height 7 ft (200cm).

Crab apple *(Malus)* – long branches heavily loaded with yellow-gold, cherry-sized fruit in autumn; it provides stunning structural stems for large arrangements. Height 33 ft (10m).

OPPOSITE, CLOCKWISE FROM LEFT: Snowberry; hawthorn; foraged rose hips; crab apple.

Foraging

While living in London and hunting down our dream cottage in the country, my husband and I used to spend weekends whizzing down country lanes doing drive-bys of potential homes. Each trip I'd raid the hedgerows for the season's bounty: a pile of lichen-covered twigs, an arching stem of rose hips, or a tangle of old man's beard (*Clematis vitalba*) to bring back to our tiny flat. Now that we're settled in our country cottage, I'm lucky enough to be able to forage for all these wild ingredients right outside our front door.

FORAGING TIPS

❋ Wear sturdy waterproof shoes – you might be climbing into ditches to collect your prizes.

❋ Use clean, sharp pruning shears.

❋ Go in early morning, when the plants are at their most hydrated, and take a bucket with some water to put the flowers in straight away after picking.

❋ On public land, it's not normally an offense to pick the "four Fs" (fruit, foliage, fungi, and flowers) if the plants are growing wild and it is for your personal use and not for sale.

❋ If you want to forage on privately owned land, you need permission from the landowner; if in doubt, always ask.

❋ Don't pick too much from one area – a little here and there lessens the impact and won't leave any gaping holes.

❋ Be mindful of impacting someone else's beauty – don't harvest close to a house where the residents might cherish glancing on a certain something every day.

❋ Leave anything that is protected, endangered, or rare well alone and never dig anything up.

❋ Condition the flowers properly – many are prone to wilting and won't last long so a little care helps.

SPRING

There are rich pickings to be had in spring as the vivid green leaves of hawthorn and beech unfurl and the hedgerows become a froth of blossom. I pick armloads of cow parsley (*Anthriscus sylvestris*) – this native wild flower looks fabulous in a vase all on its own, but needs to be conditioned properly (see Searing, page 229) or it doesn't last. I feel like I've hit the jackpot when I come across lilac (*Syringa*) and snowball bush (*Viburnum opulus* 'Roseum') with its pom-poms of greeny white flowers.

SUMMER

With so much going on in my own garden, I tend not to look elsewhere for extras in summer, although I'll sometimes venture out for additional structural branches that my newly planted garden can't provide. Anything is fair game, and I'll always try something once. I'll help myself to a few spires of buddleja if I see it swaying in the hedgerows. Ox-eye daisies (*Leucanthemum vulgare*) are also a delight.

AUTUMN

Autumn is prime foraging time for me – there's so much on offer. I use old man's beard with its long, silky, tufted balls to twist into wreaths (spray with hairspray to help the seed pods last). The hedgerows are full of rosehips – strip off any leaves and then dry in a cool, dark place to help stop them shrivelling. Hawthorn (*Crataegus monogyna*), the classic hedgerow plant with white blossom in spring, gives us red berries in autumn, but watch out for the thorns. I'm lucky enough to have a field maple (*Acer campestre*) opposite our cottage, and I love bringing

CLOCKWISE FROM TOP LEFT: A bucket of foraged autumnal foliage; cow parsley growing rampantly in the hedgerows near my house; foraged stems of rosehips and leafy branches in autumnal hues add a seasonal feel to the pickings from my cutting garden.

in the leaves as they start to take on autumnal coppers and bronzes. Then there are wild blackberries (*Rubus fruticosus*) – when picked before they ripen, they look fantastic in a mixed arrangement.

WINTER

Foliage in the cutting garden can be a bit slim in winter, so I have to hunt greenery down farther afield. Ivy (*Hedera*) is always useful to create trails in a vase or as a base for a garland or a wreath. Look for older stems with berries, which form in late summer and look fantastic as they turn black in winter. In late winter, the catkins of alder (*Alnus*), hazel (*Corylus avellana*), and willow (*Salix*) start to appear; they look stunning arranged in a vase by themselves. I make most of my wreaths from foraged vines, bendy stems, and branches, harvested in early winter before the stems go brittle so they can be twisted into shape.

6 Harvesting & arranging

Enjoying the fruits of your labor

I've spent the past 20 years styling and art directing shoots for magazines, creating images that are picture perfect. Flowers are central to conjuring up the right "feel" for an image; they add a sense of life and energy and help bring seasonality and an element of nature to a space. Blooms play the same role in real life – they make a room feel alive and cared for.

When I'm styling my home, I find that arranging flowers is one of the most enjoyable parts, but it's not about perfection, and nor are my arrangements big, elaborate numbers. I try to make flowers part of everyday life, not just for special occasions. However, I haven't got hours on end to spend styling flowers at home, so I like to keep things relatively simple and let the flowers speak for themselves.

PRACTICAL TRICKS

In this chapter, I'll share the practical tricks I've learned that work well for me: how I harvest and extend the vase life of the blooms I've picked. I'll focus on the arrangements that I use the most, the ones that are quick and easy – I think they'll probably be the ones you'll end up using most, too. Unlike other floristry books, these arrangements aren't set out as recipes as such – they are more a starting point to help you head off in the right direction using your favorite flowers in the quantities that you have growing.

It was important to me that the arrangements in this book were put together in the same way that you would do at home and show real-life displays captured by me in my home (without the usual team involved on a photographic shoot). I wanted to do things as you would be doing them in your home – my aim being to show you that if I can do it, so can you. If you look closely, you'll see weeds in the borders, leaves and petals that have been nibbled and munched – you might even spot the odd bug or two. The flaws, the mistakes, they're all part of the process.

HARVESTING

It's best to pick flowers first thing in the morning or else late in the day when it's cool and the flowers are their most hydrated. If you harvest in the heat of the day, the blooms are much more likely to wilt. Usually, I pick in the evening, strip the leaves off and condition overnight, then put any arrangements together the next morning or that evening. You'll find the rhythm that works for you.

THE RIGHT STAGE TO PICK

Generally, you want to be picking when the blooms are in their early stages – out of the tight bud stage with the flowers just opening but not fully opened with visible pollen. For spire-shaped flowers, wait until about half of the blooms have opened. Some of the flowers in this book are best when picked at a particular stage – I've made notes on those in the relevant plant entries.

HOW TO PICK

Most of the time, I'll have a bucket of water beside me to put the cut stems in straight away. If you want to save yourself a bit of hassle, strip the leaves off the stems as you pick and put them into an empty bucket or plastic bin, so they can go directly on the compost heap. The stem-clearing job is then all done before you even make it indoors.

HOW OFTEN TO CUT

In the height of the season, I'll be picking flowers about twice a week to keep the garden productive – most annuals need harvesting regularly to keep the blooms coming or they will go to seed. Keep your tools sharp to ensure any cuts you make are clean and always cut just above a new leaf bud or pair of side shoots, as this is where the new growth (and blooms) will come from.

ABOVE: A late summer picking of zinnias, sunflowers, dahlias, gladioli, bishop's flower, and grasses
LEFT: Harvesting cosmos, deadheading as I go.

CONDITIONING

Florists condition the flowers they sell to extend their vase life, and you can do the same with your garden-gathered blooms. It's a simple process where the stems are stripped of some of their leaves, freshly cut, and placed in water with flower food to rest for a few hours, ideally overnight.

❋ Keep everything clean. Use a little bleach (a drop rather than a glug) or baby sterilizer liquid and hot water to clean everything thoroughly before you use it. Any bacteria that's left lurking in vases or vessels or buckets will shorten the lifespan of your plants. If you wouldn't drink out of the vase, it's not clean enough.

❋ Use flower food. I used to fling that little packet of powdered food that comes with store-bought bouquets straight in the bin until a florist friend persuaded me that such food actually worked. It does, so don't skip this vital step. Add it to both the water you condition the flowers in and to the vase. You can make your own easily and it's just as good as store bought (see page 229).

❋ Fill your buckets with water at a temperature to suit the flowers. Most spring bulbs prefer cold water, the majority of flowers like cool water while woody stems do best in tepid water. If you have a bucket of mixed flowers, use cool water.

❋ Strip off all the leaves that will sit below the water level in the vase – this will decrease the amount of potential bacteria in the water

❋ Cut the stems at an angle. This gives the flower more surface area to soak up the water and also stops the stem from sitting flat on the surface, where it won't be able to absorb as much water

❋ Condition stems for at least a few hours – overnight if you can.

❋ Once arranged, keep the flowers out of direct sunlight, away from a heat source, and well clear of the fruit bowl. A ripe banana will "ripen" your flowers in the same way as it does a green tomato. Monitor water levels and fill regularly. Change the water completely if there's a whiff of anything untoward.

ABOVE LEFT: I always take a bucket of water out to pick with me. I hit the jackpot when I went foraging and came across the viburnum and lilac. I've added some apple blossom from my tree to the mix.
ABOVE RIGHT: The finished hand-tied posy of perennial stocks, mixed roses with bells of Ireland, and bishop's flower as fillers and a few grasses for texture.
OPPOSITE: Getting ready to make a small, hand-tied posy – all stems are stripped of the bottom 6–8 in (15–20cm) of foliage and laid out. I try to keep roses out of water as little as possible when arranging.

STEM PREPARATION

Most flowers are happy with a diagonal cut at the base of their stem and a night spent in a bucket of water with flower food. However, some blooms aren't quite as easygoing and need a little extra care. The requirements depend on the type of stem they have: woody, milky, hollow, or soft. I've mentioned in the notes under each flower in the plant chapters if the blooms need any special treatment.

The most common cause of wilting in cut flowers is because of an airlock – a bubble of air trapped in the stem that stops water from reaching the flower head. Stem preparation is all about reducing the chances of creating an airlock and increasing the uptake of water

"SEARING"

Some flowers such as Icelandic poppies, hellebores, and avens last longer in the vase if you sear the stems before conditioning. There are two ways to do this: by placing the freshly cut stems in just-boiled water for 20–30 seconds (take care that you don't steam the flower heads); or by holding the stem in a flame from a match or a candle for 30 seconds. Condition as normal afterwards.

Daffodils and narcissi exude a milky sap and need to be conditioned for 12 hours in tepid water to halt the sap – do this separately as other flowers find this sap poisonous, then arrange as normal. Make sure you cut your flowers to their final length before you condition, as recutting will start the sap flowing again.

WATER-FILLING HOLLOW STEMS

Some florists condition hollow-stemmed flowers such as delphiniums, dahlias, and amaryllis by filling them with water. They turn the stem upside down and pour water in, and then either plug the stem with some cotton wool, or put their thumb over it and release once the stem is back in the water. This seems like a lot of extra work to me, so I've rarely ever done this, and I've had no major issues with the vase life of any of these types of flowers.

THE "V" CUT FOR WOODY STEMS

Lilacs, magnolia, spring blossom, and all other plants that make you reach for your shears when harvesting need the base of each stem cut with an upward-facing "V." This creates more surface area to absorb water. Condition as normal in tepid water rather than cold.

MAKE YOUR OWN FLOWER FOOD

Add 1 teaspoon of sugar, 1 teaspoon of bleach, and 2 teaspoons of vinegar to 2 pints (1⅛ liters) of lukewarm water. The bleach is there to keep the bacteria at bay, the vinegar is to acidify the alkaline tap water to speed up water absorption, and the sugar is there to feed the flowers.

HARVESTING FOR DRYING

For a modern take on dried flowers, look for interesting sculptural varieties to dry, to use as a textural addition in a mixed fresh arrangement, or as a styling element in its own right rather than trying to mimic a fresh arrangement in dry materials. Celebrate the airiness and lightness – there's a beauty in the fragility..

❋ Keep out of sunlight once the stems are cut, to maintain color. A position in the dark but still warm, with good circulation, is good. I dry mine hanging from the rafters in my garden shed in summer.

❋ Most blooms can be tied in a bunch and hung upside down, but some flowers, such as love-lies-bleeding, with its long heavy tassels, are best left in an empty vase to dry, to preserve the natural beauty of their form.

RESCUING WILTED FLOWERS

If you get to them in time, wilted flowers can be revived using the water-searing method. This stem of 'Koko Loko' roses (pictured above) was above the waterline in an arrangement for a few days before I spotted they had wilted. I thought they'd gone beyond the point of no return, but was pleasantly surprised to see them come back to life overnight after searing. You should be able to spot little bubbles in the water as they escape from the airlock.

The tool kit for floristry

Behind every good professional stylist there's a tool kit full of tricks of the trade – I have one especially for flower arranging, packed with all sorts of ribbons and twine, wire and tape alongside my favorite flower snips and scissors. You could quite feasibly get away with just a decent pair of scissors and pruning shears – to ensure your cuts are clean to extend the vase life of your flowers. But if you want to make the most of your garden-gathered blooms and take your arrangements to the next level, it's worth investing in a basic kit of your own.

Flower scissors: normal scissors aren't geared up for stems and can crush rather than cut and so prevent proper water uptake. Keep flower scissors sharp for the same reason.

Pruning shears: use these to cut cleanly through tough stems when scissors aren't suitable for the job. Never leave any jagged edges, which encourage bacteria and kill your flowers off quickly.

Wire cutters: you need a special tool for cutting wire. Don't just use your scissors or pruning shears – you'll ruin them.

Wire: if you're going to be making wreaths or bowers or any of the more involved arrangements in this book, you'll need wire. I use it on a reel for attaching moss to wreath frames, and stick (or stub) wire for everything else.

String: for tying up bouquets, string is invaluable. Watch out for colored string as it might color the water if it's not colorfast.

Flower frogs: also called pin holders, usually made up of a series of brass pins set into a metal base. You place one at the bottom of the vase, secure with florists' tack, and then push the bottom of the flower stems into the pins to anchor them in place. I use these as an alternative to floral foam to help prevent flowers from flopping out to the sides. I have 2 in (5cm) and 4 in (10cm) diameter sizes.

Floral tape: to secure a flower frog in place at the bottom of the vase, use floral tape, which has the texture of putty. If your flower frog is quite heavy, you might be able to get away without the tape.

Florists' pot tape: a super-strong, waterproof sticky tape that is ideal for securing chickenwire inside pots and to create a criss-cross support system for stems over the opening of a vase. It can also be used to bunch flowers together.

Chicken wire: this is especially useful when arranging large displays to help stabilize the stems. It needs to be molded into a ball and positioned in the vase.

Ribbons, sheets of tissue, rolls of paper: if you want to give your flowers as gifts, you need a range of attractive paper and ribbons for wrapping.

Buckets, large jugs, watertight containers: I take buckets/ containers filled with water out to the garden to put the flowers in right away when I pick. I have a selection of vessels of different sizes to suit different flowers; don't bundle them all in one bucket if you can help it – the short or delicate flowers can often get squashed by taller or more robust flowers or tend to slide down the side of the bucket becoming submerged in the water. I try to keep them separate as much as I can.

Styling your bounty

How you arrange your flowers depends on your personal style, what you're growing, and how much time you have. My aim here is to cover the basic techniques – the ones I use time and time again both at home and on my shoots at work. I approach putting flowers together in a few different ways. Each depends on the look and feel, shape, and scale of the arrangement, the size of vase, and the type of flowers I'm working with. I generally put the flowers together in my hand, building up an arrangement known as a "hand-tied" or else construct it in the vase freestyle, stem by stem.

THE MECHANICS OF AN ARRANGEMENT

The main thing to consider when arranging flowers is how are you going to stop the stems from splaying out to the edges of the container and leaving a sorry-looking hole in the middle of the arrangement. There are a few different techniques I use to deal with this. The choice of vase helps: a vessel with a narrow neck holds the stems closely together, while a wider-necked one allows them to splay out (see page 236).

❋ **Cutting short and packing flowers closely together:** Allowing flowers to rub shoulders with one another means they become self-supporting once they're in the vase and so won't splay out as much. The shorter you cut the stems, the fewer flowers you'll need to fill out a vase. I use my flowers surprisingly short, ignoring all traditional arranging rules about proportion. For a quick display, I'll arrange the flowers in my hand in a bunch, cut the stems to length, and then plonk them in the vase, gently releasing my grip at the last minute once all the stems are safely in.

❋ **Securing the stems together:** I'll sometimes tie an elastic band around the stems to keep them together. It can be moved up and down the stems easily to alter the shape the flower heads' form. The higher the band, the tighter together the flower heads will be; the lower, the farther apart. This tip works best when you're using just one type of flower – or flowers that have the same stem thickness.

❋ **Arranging as hand-tied:** A hand-tied arrangement can be as small as a posy or big enough to fill a large pickle jar. As the arrangement is being put together in your hand, you turn it periodically so that when you've finished there's a spiral formation to the stems and they can be tied together where you've been holding the arrangement and the whole thing will stay put. It's really just the same principle as the elastic band. By twisting the stems you help to keep the flowers nicely spaced – the higher up the stems you hold while building the arrangement, the closer together the flowers will be (see page 243).

❋ **Using strong stems as "scaffolding":** It's possible to use sturdy stems as a base or framework to support the others and stop them from flopping out. Arrange the stronger stems first, then fill in with the other flowers, resting the weaker ones within the stronger.

OPPOSITE, CLOCKWISE FROM TOP LEFT: The sturdy stems of copper beech create a "scaffolding" to support the other stems. (I used the same basic ingredients for each of the displays here and the following two pages – adjusting stem length as required): 'Nicholas' dahlias, 'Wollerton Old Hall' roses, copper beech, weeping birch, apple branches, and northern sea oats grass; the flowers in this mug were cut short and packed closely together so that they became self-supporting.

Using sticky tape: Lengths of sticky tape or florists' pot tape applied over the top of the vase opening in criss-crosses creates a grid that will help to support the flowers. The flowers are inserted into the squares, and the tape holds the stems more upright.

Flower frogs: A flower frog (see page 230) allows you to position flower stems in isolation exactly where you want them. It's perfect for small- to medium-scale arrangements. I'll use one when the shape of the vase doesn't allow me to use other methods of support or when I want an arrangement with lots of space between the stems for a light and airy feel.

Chicken wire: A piece of chicken wire (see page 230) scrunched up and made into a ball so that it fits into your vase is an excellent way of creating support for stems, whether the arrangement is small or large. It's an excellent alternative to floral foam.

Florists' water tubes: Re-useable plastic vials with a removable rubber top that once filled with water will keep a single stem hydrated. I use them when making wreaths and garlands to keep flowers fresh.

ABOVE: Apple and copper beech branches form the base of this display with the jug arrangement creating the floral focal point. OPPOSITE: The same apple branches give heigh and structure to this large urn display. BELOW: Chicken wire is used to help support t stems in the urn.

A word on vases

The feel of an arrangement, as well its scale and shape are greatly influenced by the vessel you choose. Many people think they're no good at arranging flowers, but often it's just that they've been using an inappropriate vase. Choose the right vase for the job and arranging becomes a breeze.

❋ **Pickle jars:** The one vase I come back to again and again is a pickle jar, as it's so versatile. Some are designed with a small opening, which means the flowers don't splay out too much. They're great for large, relaxed arrangements.

❋ **Votives, tumblers, short glasses, jam jars, etc.:** Your kitchen cupboards are probably full of these. I reach for them the most as they are ideal for the small- to medium-size posies that I make all the time. I use them by themselves or in clusters for more impact. I collect all our glass jars to reuse as vases for the flowers I give away as presents.

❋ **Bud vases:** I use this as a generic term to cover all manner of bottles and containers that have a narrow opening at the top. Bud vases are handy to set in rows as decorations down a dining table or along a mantlepiece, without taking up too much space. The mini, clear-glass, milk-bottle style ones come in really handy in installations

– they are discreet enough to hide among foliage and flowers, while providing water for stems that need it.

❋ **Cylinder vases:** These are straight up and down and take a lot of flowers to fill and look generous. I use them for flowers with lots of foliage that look good when tightly packed together, such as tulips.

❋ **Urns:** These are wider at the top with a generous opening, which makes them perfect for large arrangements. Choose one in metal – the extra weight will help keep it from tipping over if you're using heavy plant material.

❋ **One-offs:** Pick these up as and when you come across one that appeals to you, to build up a collection that's unique to you.

✻ **Bowls:** I raid the kitchen all the time for vessels. I use large serving bowls to plant up potted arrangements – lining them with plastic to protect their inside. I use smaller bowls for ikebana-inspired arrangements with either a flower frog or a small ball of chicken wire to support the stems.

✻ **Crates, wooden boxes, and buckets:** If rustic is your thing, then a couple of vintage crates or boxes will come in handy. I use the larger ones for potted arrangements and the smaller ones to group together jam-jar displays. I'll often use the buckets I've conditioned flowers in, to display them as well – they look too good to dismantle sometimes.

SEE EVERYTHING AS A VASE

Nearly every type of vessel can be a vase; if it's hollow, it can be a vase. Even if something isn't watertight, you can always pop a waterproof container inside to hold the water – a plastic bottle with the top cut down or a tumbler will work.

Keeping it simple

If you're completely new to flower arranging, it can be a little daunting knowing where to start, but stunning displays needn't be complicated. A few choice blooms nestled in a vase can be a thing of beauty.

PICK & PLONK

It doesn't get much easier than this. One type of bloom, one vase. No arranging to speak of – just cut the stems to height and position in your vase of choice.

STYLING TIPS

❋ Consider how the size of vase neck or opening will affect how the flowers sit within it. I use pickle jars with a narrow neck for long stems; tumblers or votives when I'm using only a few short stems and want something small; and I'll choose a wide-necked vase such as an urn or a bucket when I'm feeling extravagant and want to pick an armload of something.

❋ Generally, because you're using one type of flower, the stems should look neat and tidy, so you can select a glass vessel and not have to really worry about having unsightly, straggly stems on view.

❋ Don't be afraid to cut short. You might be surprised by how short you might need to go.

TOP: 'Aveyron' and 'Copper Image' tulips massed together in a small jug.
BOTTOM: The soft muted pinks of a tumbler full of mixed pink roses complements the delicate peach of 'Sutton's Apricot' foxgloves.
OPPOSITE: A mug filled with mixed dahlias cut super-short – 'Edge of Joy' and 'Thomas A. Eddison'.

THE FLOWER MARKET/
FLORIST SHOP LOOK

A high-end flower shop is one of my favorite spaces to be. Florist extraordinaire Vic Brotherson of Scarlet & Violet has created one of my favorite happy places in London, and La Boutique des Saint-Pères in Paris is one I try to fit in when I'm there. The beauty and magic come not only from the stunning varieties the designers have selected, but also from the feeling of sheer abundance. You can recreate this at home (albeit on a much smaller scale) without needing to work that hard. It happens almost by default as you harvest and group your flowers together for conditioning.

STYLING TIPS

❀ There's nothing involved in this other than separating the flowers by type or height when you condition them and finding appropriately sized vessels to put them in – something I do anyway as I prepare to start arranging and that you will probably do, too.

❀ This look works best if you treat yourself to pretty containers and buckets to sit the blooms in. Use a few vases and jugs in the mix, for shorter stems to go in.

OPPOSITE: A midsummer harvest of roses, sweet peas, larkspur, scabious, dahlias, and the first trails of love-in-a-puff and dahlias alongside fillers including bishop's flower, wild carrot, and foliage, such as borage, salvia, and honeywort.
ABOVE: Mini buckets are ideal to use for conditioning shorter-stemmed flowers like sweet peas.
LEFT: Cornflower 'Classic Magic'.

Arranging in the hand

The majority of my everyday flower displays are put together in the hand (as opposed to building them stem by stem in the vase). It's the quickest way to achieve a mixed bunch and gives you the freedom to change things as you go along. They can be as simple as a posy of foraged wildflowers arranged on the way home to a more elaborate mixed bouquet for a friend's birthday – master the basic techniques and you won't look back.

THE HAND-TIED POSY

This works on the same principle as the no-tie posy (page 244), but it's the way a florist would do it. It involves turning the bunch as you make it so that the stems create a spiral. This makes it a little neater and holds together better. This posy can work for anything from a small-scale display to a showstopper – basically it's as many stems as you can grip in one hand. It might feel a bit fiddly to make the first few times, but it will get easier with practice.

HOW TO

❀ Have all your conditioned flowers and foliage laid out and ready to use. Strip off any leaves that remain on the bottom 6 in (15cm) of the stems and any thorns.

❀ I normally start off a hand-tied posy in the same way as a no-tie posy: with a stem of soft foliage (or three if they are small) and a focal flower, then I add some filler, then a secondary flower and then continue with the rest. I'm right-handed and I hold the arrangement in my left hand, adding new stems with my right. Switch over if you're left-handed.

❀ Every third stem or so, you turn the bunch in your hand. Keeping the stems facing the same direction, add another three stems and turn again, and so on. The spiral formation will begin to happen. As you continue adding flowers, position them a little lower so that you get a nice rounded shape.

❀ For a slightly wilder feel to your bunch, pull a few of the flowers a little higher out of the main bunch. I find this works best with the smaller, wiry-stemmed flowers,

OPPOSITE: A work in progress;
a hand-tied bouquet of dahlias,
copper beech, and cosmos.
ABOVE: An autumnal bunch of
hydrangeas and sunflowers (stripped
of their petals) with copper beech.

to add a little quirk. Once you're happy, tie the bunch with string where you've been holding it and secure with a double knot.

STYLING TIPS

❀ The height at which you hold the bunch when arranging affects how close the flowers are together. If you want a more relaxed open bunch, hold the stems lower down. If you prefer something a little denser, hold them nearer their heads. I find working in front of mirror helps – you can see how the bunch is coming together much more easily.

THE NO-TIE POSY

Aka, the arrange-and-plonk technique, it's the quickest, easiest way to create a mixed bouquet. It's best for small arrangements and for designs where the flowers and foliage will be nestled closely together.

HOW TO

❋ Get ready with all your conditioned flowers and foliage laid out and ready to use. Strip off any leaves that will be below the waterline in your vase. I normally start off the posy with a stem of soft foliage (or three if they are small) and a focal flower, then I'll add some filler, then a secondary flower and then a bit more foliage and so on, until I'm pleased with how it's looking. I'm right-handed and I hold the arrangement in my left hand, adding new stems with my right. Switch over if you're left-handed.

❋ If I'm keeping the stems long, I'll finish off by adding some foliage to the outsides of the posy to soften how it sits in the vase. This also helps to hide the edge of the vase. If the posy is going to be ultra-short, I don't bother.

❋ Once I'm happy with the results, I'll cut the stems to the length I want, then hold the posy up to the vase to check the length.

❋ Then I'll ease the posy into the vase and gently let go.

STYLING TIPS

❋ The beauty of not tying the bouquet is that you can tweak it really easily once it's in the vase if something does not look quite right or you need to add something extra. In a no-tie arrangement, I'll often wait until the end to add that little bit of magic – a wiggly stem or a trailing bit of foliage.

❋ Don't feel that things always need to be symmetrical and form a tidy dome shape. I'll often weight the display to one side to knock off the symmetry so that there's a sense of movement through the arrangement.

❋ Stems can look messy as there's no pretty twisting technique here to show off, so you might want to use an opaque vessel. I used glass vases here so that you could see what things looked like.

OPPOSITE LEFT: A little wild: This early spring arrangement of hellebores and fritillaries has a wild, organic feel to it and is only possible as a no-tie posy because the sturdy stems of hawthorn and blossom give the other flowers support. I held the stems quite low down as I was putting together this arrangement and left some of the stems extra-long so that it had a looser feel and gave the hellebores and fritillaries a chance to arch gracefully.

OPPOSITE RIGHT: Foxglove and roses.

ABOVE: Playing with symmetry: An early summer arrangement of 'Harry Edland' and 'Blue For You' roses with love-in-a-mist, bishop's flower, and sweet william. The flowers are tightly packed together and give each other support. I added the stems of copper beech and love-in-a-mist in bud at the last minute to break up the dome shape and pulled out the stem with a cluster of roses to knock the symmetry off-center.

Building a display stem by stem

When creating a large-scale arrangement or something where I want more control, I'll build it in the vase rather than in my hand. There are various techniques you can use to help support the stems, depending on the vessel you're using.

USING STURDY STEMS AS SCAFFOLDING – THE PICKLE JAR DISPLAY

Sturdy, comparatively robust flower stems can be positioned in such a way that they support each other and other flowers – you shouldn't need to use any other support for the stems. Choosing a vase with a narrow neck such as a pickle jar will make things easier as the stems won't splay out so much.

HOW TO

❋ Start with all your conditioned flowers and foliage laid out. Strip off any leaves that still remain from the bottom two-thirds or so of the stems.

❋ Arrange the sturdiest stems first. These are usually the structural foliage, such as catkins, in a small pickle jar, but in the large pickle jar display opposite it was the foxgloves. I arranged them with their stems criss-crossing over one another to create a "nest" for the other flowers.

❋ Then add any other foliage and fillers to create the base of your arrangement.

❋ Next it's time for your "flowers." I start with the heroes, positioning them where I want the focal point and then adding the secondary ones. In this large pickle jar, it's the peonies as hero and mock orange as secondary.

❋ Tweak things as you go. I moved the central foxglove over to the left as I felt it was looking too straight, then had to make the bellflowers more upright to fill the gap that moving the foxglove had created. Pull and tease stems out a little to vary the heights, but make sure they remain in the water – add more if you need to.

❋ It's at this point that I sometimes add a little trail of something or a stem that will spill over the edge, to make the composition feel a little "unmade."

OPPOSITE: For this arrangement, I used foxgloves as the sturdy stems (as well as a focal flower) with peonies as an additional focal flower, then bellflowers and mock orange as secondary flowers, hare's ear as a filler, and sweeping stems of weeping birch and arches of bishop's flower to add a sense of movement.

USING A MASS OF STEMS AS A "NEST" – THE URN DISPLAY

This is another of my "cheat" arrangements. I use this one when I need something big and showy, but don't have the time for something more intricate. The display looks as if you've spent ages on it, but in fact it takes about ten minutes to create.

HOW TO

✻ For this, choose a vessel such as this small urn, which tapers slightly toward the top to let the flowers fall out a little to the sides, but still has a relatively small space for the stems to sit within, so they end up being closely packed together. The arrangement is constructed on the same principle as the smaller no-tie posy (see page 244), in that the tightly packed stems (here, the foliage base) become self-supporting.

✻ The metal urn I used has a hole at the bottom, so I slipped a tall glass jar inside to make it waterproof.

✻ I wanted a lush, full arrangement with a soft, frothy feel, and for it I had plenty of bells of Ireland to pick – many of which had started to lean after being flattened by a downpour. I used about 20 stems to form the apple-green base that would work as the "nest" to support the other stems. I started off by arranging these in my hand, creating a big bunch, with the stems around the outside a little shorter than those toward the center. I cut the stems to length, then positioned the stems in the urn and gently let go, allowing them to fall naturally. I love the way the some of the stems splayed out at the edges, especially the ones that weren't picked as perfect poker-straight stems.

✻ Fill in any gaps that might have opened up with additional stems of base foliage. I like to pull out a few of the stems a little here and there, to give it a slightly wilder feel. At this point, I made sure all the stems were still in water – add more water or push the stems in a little if you need to.

✻ Add your hero and secondary flowers – sliding them in among the base foliage. Things may move slightly, but that's ok – it all adds to the natural feel. I find creating an imaginary "triangle" with a hero flower at each corner seems to make a pleasing shape. If your arrangement is going against a wall, don't waste flowers at the back – position them toward the front and the side.

✻ Once the flowers are in place, it's time to add the fillers

ABOVE: A base of bells of Ireland created the "nest," *hydrangea paniculata* acted as hero, with secondary flowers of 'Tranquility' rose. Fillers of Panicum 'Frosted Explosion', bishop's flower, and foxtail grass and copper beech were added to create arches and trails. OPPOSITE: Laying out the ingredients beforehand makes arranging much easier.

for extra texture and to fill in any gaps. I used a little bit of bishop's flower and four stems of *Panicum* 'Frosted Explosion' grass. You can cheat with the grass and position it where you like, as it lasts so well out of water. Just strip the leaves so they don't wilt.

❋ Then it's time to add the final flourishes: a few arching stems to create a sense of movement (the foxtail grass), or a wiry stem popping out (the scabious seedhead on the left), or some trailing foliage (the copper beech) – all of which should slide in easily and stay put.

STABILIZING THE STEMS

Bells of Ireland has quite a robust structure and works brilliantly as a "nest," but if you are using something a little less dense you might need to wedge a small ball of chicken wire in the base of the urn so that you're able to anchor the sturdier-stemmed flowers at the base and they don't squash the lighter flowers, but still have the joy of the natural movement at the top.

USING CHICKEN WIRE — THE SPRAY

A fan-shaped vase is wide and open and allows you to create a wild and free flowing arrangement incorporating lots of material. In a display like this I find the best way to support the stems is to use chicken wire formed into a ball or oval shape placed tightly into the vase.

HOW TO

❋ First, mold your ball or oval of chicken wire to fit the shape of your vase. Hold it in place with florist pot tape.

❋ Start by adding the structural foliage to create the framework – here it was the burgundy ninebark and silver-gray daisy bush – I also added foraged blackberries at this point as a decorative filler. Allow the stems to cascade over the front and sides of the vase to create a sense of flow and movement.

❋ Once you are happy with the overall shape that these stems have created, add your focal flowers – here I used a mix of roses. I positioned them so that some sat closely to the vase, but others flowed up and out to create a sense of direction. Allow any natural curves in the stems to lead you. I find it works better when I cluster a few together rather than spreading them all out.

❋ Then it's time to add the contrasting flowers – here, instead of flowers, I used foxtail grass, as I liked the movement of its arched growth habitat. Other spires and spikes like snapdragons or larkspur would have worked well here.

❋ I then added *Panicum* 'Frosted Explosion' grasses to act as a filler to close up any gaps – they also add height and texture.

❋ I added a last-minute stem of dahlia that reaches out toward the left, I felt that the leading flower was too much, so I snipped that off and left the two flower buds to do the job themselves.

❋ As a final flourish, I added a little texture with some dried larkspur as I had some handy and thought it balanced the stronger pink of the rose on the right.

STYLING TIPS

❋ Don't worry about symmetry or things being uneven; flowers at different heights, stems cascading over the edges, a puff of grass heading in one direction – they're all part of making your display look untamed and informal.

❋ Think of shape, texture, and form (look back to Chapter 1 for a reminder). Use fillers to add airiness, spires and spikes to add height, secondary flowers for a change of pace, and a hero to create a focal point. Foliage creates the backdrop as well as softening the edges of the vessel.

OPPOSITE: Roses take center stage in this arrangement, with mixed grasses and dried larkspur providing texture and flow with their gentle arches and frothy explosions.

USING A FLOWER FROG — THE BOWL

In this small bowl arrangement, I was aiming for a display where I could position the stems exactly where I wanted and give the flowers a chance to breathe. A flower frog (or pin holder) is ideal for giving the stems support in this situation – or you could use a small piece of chicken wire.

HOW TO

❋ Without something to support the flower stems, it would be almost impossible to display flowers like this in a shallow bowl – they would just splay out and collapse. A flower frog makes it possible. Choose one that fits snuggly in the vessel and secure it in position with floral tape. I sometimes use chicken wire taped into place when I don't have a flower frog that will fit, but the ball of chicken wire can slip and move sometimes – depending on the flowers I'm using.

❋ Start by adding the main foliage stems (ninebark and copper beech in this display) to create the backdrop for your flowers – use them to create the overall shape of the display and to cover up the base of the bowl to hide all your mechanics.

❋ Then add your soft or secondary foliage (the coral bells here) and filler – I used some autumnal-colored hydrangea to create a "dome" around the bowl to visually "anchor" the display.

❋ Next, add your focal flowers – I used very little in this display, just one sprig of *Hydrangea arborescens* 'Sweet Annabelle' and a 'Lady of Shallot' rose, as this arrangement is really about celebrating the beauty of autumnal foliage rather than the flowers.

❋ To finish off, add any final flourishes – I added a wiry stem of scabious seed pod.

STYLING TIPS

❋ Focus on the natural movement of the stems and branches you are using – let them guide you.

❋ Keep things loose and let the flowers breathe – don't be tempted to keep everything in a tight dome. It's ok to have stems that wiggle up and out, heading off in one direction all on their own – that's all part of the look.

❋ Displaying in a bowl like this makes a showcase out of the smallest flowers – I'll often use up leftovers in this way. This is also a great way to decorate a table – as you can create lots of interest at a low level without obscuring people's view of one another.

ABOVE: A flower frog or chicken wire secured in the bowl helps keep the stems in place.
OPPOSITE TOP: The foliage of ninebark, copper beech, and coral bells forms the basic structure and shape.
OPPOSITE BOTTOM: The hydrangeas and roses are added last.

A cluster of bud vases

There's always something in the garden you can pop into a few bud vases. I'm using the term "bud vase" here to cover all manner of single-stem vases and little bottles with narrow necks – your kitchen cupboards will be full of them. I've amassed a collection over the years that work well together – from simple mini glass bottles to engraved crystal and handblown glass. Look for colors, textures, and shapes that all combine and blend well together.

I'll either dot a few of the vases singly about the house – on a bedside table, a bookshelf, at the bathroom sink, or I'll cluster them together en masse along a mantelpiece or down the center of a table. It's such an easy way of creating something beautiful out of very little material as it becomes so much more than the sum of its parts.

I'll often use the odds and ends I might have left over from making up other arrangements as well as putting any garden casualties to good use; a hollyhock cut short by a stray football, or a flower that wasn't staked properly and is a little too wiggly for a taller display. It's a chance to showcase nature and the individuality of each flower – their bends and twists and nodding heads all adding to the look. If I'm arranging them in a group, I'll treat the vases as a whole, filling them with water, positioning and then arranging the flowers as one big arrangement. That way you get a nice flow and sense of movement as stems weave in and out of one another.

STYLING TIPS

✻ The narrow necks of bud vases suit wiry, wispy stems if you want height with a nicely angled stem.

✻ Thicker, sturdier stems are better cut short or used one or two per vessel so they aren't forced to become too upright.

✻ The more stems you try and fit into a bud vase, the closer together they become and the more upright they'll be.

RIGHT: Stems of larkspur, snapdragons, and dahlias in vintage glass bottles.
OPPOSITE: A mix of cosmos, grasses, and roses including the lilac 'Harry Edland', buff-colored 'Koko Loko' and coral 'Duchess of Cornwall'.

A cheat's garland

This one is a really easy way to create a linear display in very little time. I've used this method on most of my Christmas decorating shoots when there just isn't the time to wire everything in properly as a florist would. It works either as a table runner for a dining centerpiece or as decoration along a mantlepiece or shelf.

HOW TO

❋ Choose a base layer of foliage – here I've used climbing nasturtiums (right) and copper beech, ivy, and jasmine (opposite). Lay these out along the length of the surface you want to decorate, making sure some of the foliage is long enough to trail over the edges at either end.

❋ Some foliage lasts quite well out of water, like ivy and copper beech – long enough to get through a party. If you choose more delicate foliage and want the display to last, the trick is to use small, clear, milk-bottle–style vessels to hold the water for the stems that won't last without water – they are easily camouflaged with the foliage. Position the filled bottles near the ends of the stems and carefully guide the stems into them. You might have to move things a little to get the angles right; following the natural movement of the stems will help make things easier. Use a blob of floral tape on the bottom of the bottles, to secure them in place and prevent them from toppling over.

❋ Add your hero flowers. I popped a few stems of roses into each of the glass bottles in the display opposite. Because the nasturtiums I used (right) had plenty of flowers, I needed to add only a few extra dahlias to provide the color I wanted. I gave the display a little bit more height and substance by incorporating a couple of metal votives with a few more stems of nasturtiums and more dahlias (I didn't mind these being on show).

❋ I then added a few little extra flourishes – a few vines of unripened tomatoes in both displays and let them spill out of the foliage; mini pumpkins, apples, pears, or figs would all work – just use what you have on hand and what suits the color palette you're working on.

❋ This method works best when you're using foliage stems that you can either leave out of water, or you can easily coerce into the glass bottles. I sometimes use florists' water tubes for a situation where I can't use the glass bottles.

OPPOSITE: Copper beech leaves and ivy form the base of this garland, with trails of jasmine added alongside roses, green tomatoes, and apples.
BELOW: A "garland" of 'Milkmaid' nasturtiums with 'Honka Surprise' and 'Nicholas' dahlias and a scattering of green tomatoes on the vine.

ABOVE, CLOCKWISE FROM TOP LEFT:
A no-base wreath made from dried
hops; a rosemary wreath; a slow-
dry hydrangea wreath and a natural
vine wreath.
ABOVE RIGHT: A dense foliage wreath
made from yew with added grasses
and hydrangeas.
RIGHT: Building a moss base.

The wreath

There's a common misconception about wreaths – most people associate them only with the holiday season, yet they can be used year-round to decorate your home and celebrate the seasons.

THE BASE

Basically, anything round can be used as a base for a wreath: a store-bought copper wire ring; an embroidery hoop; a trail of vine teased into shape. They can all work depending on the final look you are after and which cut materials you'll be using. Alternatively, you can opt for no base at all.

No-base wreath: For a super-easy and quick wreath, you can use the foliage material itself to form the wreath without the need for a base. This works particularly well with short sprigs of woody foliage. Simply attach the sprigs to one another (facing them in the same direction) to eventually form the circle, bending them gently as you go if you need to and using wire to secure them. This method also works on a much larger scale with longer trailing stems: I like to use a length of foraged hops, teasing the vine into a circle shape and securing the ends together with wire, to create an instant wreath. .

Dense foliage wreath: For a classic wreath, primed with foliage to use as your blank canvas, you'll first need to make a moss base, which will help keep your foliage hydrated. To do this, cover a copper wreath frame (bought online) with moist sphagnum moss (from florists' supplies), packing it tightly together as you go and securing it in place with reel wire. Don't worry about the moss base being neat – it won't be seen when it's finished. Add your foliage of choice in clusters, poking the stems into the moss base and fanning the stems out to cover it, and wiring them in as you go along. The base is then ready for your floral flourishes; attach them with wire to the base. I choose flowers such as autumnal hydrangeas that will last for weeks (and eventually dry beautifully) with their stems just poked into the moist moss, or I'll use florists' water tubes that can be wired onto the wreath and filled with water.

Natural vine wreath: A few years ago, a Virginia creeper (*Parthenocissus*) was starting to take over our garden so I chopped it all back and twisted the stems into wreaths of different sizes. I still use those wreaths as a base for all sorts of displays – adding fresh flowers, sprigs of herb, or trails of climbing plants. Most climbers work: clematis,

honeysuckle, wisteria. I also forage for stems to use in autumn or early winter. You can buy natural vine wreaths ready-made.

Slow-dry wreath: It was by happy accident that I discovered this method. I made a hydrangea wreath using a moss ring as a base and filling it with autumnal hydrangea flower heads. These dried gradually and the colors faded beautifully over time (the one in the picture opposite is 11 months old). Slow drying is such a simple wreath technique and works really well with textural blooms and foliage such as hydrangeas, dusty miller, and daisy bush 'Sunshine'.

SHAPE & SIZE

Wreaths don't have to be round – they can be square, oval, heart-shaped – just watch out with letters as they can look a little funereal unless you do something very delicate. If you're making your own base, change up the scale. Going super large or dinky makes things look unique as it's difficult to buy frames in those sizes.

THE DIRECTION OF MATERIAL

Another thing to consider is the direction you place the plant material on the wreath. Do you want to start in one place and one section and continue creating a lovely flowing pattern? Or do you prefer to keep things more symmetrical and start at the bottom of the wreath and work your way up either side and meet at top? Both methods are equally valid – it depends on the final look you're after. I sometimes like to create a focal point – the obvious places are top and bottom, but I like to add flowers or other features at "2 o'clock," "4 o'clock," and "10 o'clock" as I find it more pleasing to the eye.

Curating still lifes

While the simple gesture of positioning a tumbler or jam jar with a few stems picked from the garden is enough to show a space is cared for, considered, and loved, the real joy for me comes from "playing" with the blooms and styling them within my home. Over my time as a stylist, I have worked on hundreds of shoots, nearly always with an arrangement of some kind. The styling process begins with your choice of vase and blooms, but where and how you position them and what you choose to display with them are just as important (and enjoyable) parts of the process.

STYLING TIPS

❋ Think about where your everyday floral hotspots are: bedside table, the hallway table, the coffee table. Consider the shape and style of arrangements that might look best there and how you could use the flowers you grow to style the space. Don't immediately go for a mixed posy everywhere – if you need something short and wide for a coffee table, which is best viewed from above, a cluster of tumblers filled with different flowers from your patch, cut short, then positioned together on a tray might be more interesting (and much quicker) than making a single large display. I have an upholstered ottoman that I've topped with an oversized tray that acts as a blank canvas for a "tablescape," and I fill the vessels with different flowers each week as a kind of ever-changing floral nature table.

❋ Try positioning your vase differently – go off-center – or double up and work the symmetrical thing.

❋ "Anchor" your display by positioning it in relation to other decorative elements in your home: beneath a piece of art, or just in front of a wall-hung mirror. The spacial relationship the flowers have with other elements matters as it makes the positioning feel considered. Popping a vase of flowers on top of a pile of books or a tray also anchors the display and gives it extra height. It works like a kind of 3D frame, helping to draw the eye in. The same principle works when you use a vertical element such as a decorative tray or a book behind the flowers.

❋ Think of your flowers as the leading element, and bring in other props alongside them to style your home: use a postcard, candles, or other bits and bobs. The display then becomes much more than the sum of its parts. Choose elements that sit well with the flowers because of color, feel, or vibe. Also use other organic materials alongside your blooms to enhance the display: houseplants, fruit, vegetables, or a vine of cherry tomatoes all work well and help to celebrate the variety of nature.

ABOVE: A mixed posy is "anchored" and given extra height by the vintage books.
OPPOSITE: Simple sweet peas and roses become a still life with the addition of a decorative tray, a potted succulent, and dried roses.

USING DRIED MATERIAL

Dried flowers have been going through a bit of a revival recently, but don't worry, it's not a 1980s-style flashback. Treat such dried material as another decorative element to use in a still life or tablescape, as opposed to mimicking what you would do with a fresh arrangement.

MY FAVORITES

It's worth giving most plants a try to see how they turn out – consider everything fair game: seedheads, seed pods, grasses, berries, and leaves – not just the flowers. Below are the ones I tend to use the most. For advice on harvesting for drying see page 229.

Hydrangeas: These shrubs are useful throughout the year to add to mixed arrangements and wreaths. The flower head color gently fades, but I love it even more for that. I dry heads in late summer or early autumn by popping them in a vase in the house with just 1–2 in (3–5cm) of water. I get rid of them only when I harvest the new batch the following year (see also Slow-Dry Wreath, page 259).

Honesty (*Lunaria annua*): The beautiful, glass-like seed discs can work in so many ways. They make a stunning ephemeral wreath – the stems being light enough to be displayed on a wall with a piece of sticky tape – or else you can nestle a cluster into a bouquet. The seedpods need stripping of their outer coating – just rub the disks between finger and thumb to release them.

Ornamental onions (*Allium*): I love their sculptural, firework-like spheres even more when they have gone to seed. I let them dry naturally in the garden and bring them in once their seeds have dropped so that they have the chance to self-seed and spread in my borders. Lots of people spray-paint ornamental onion seedheads, but I like them best kept in their natural state, detached from their stalk and used as decoration within a still life or tablescape.

Hops (*Humulus*): I'm lucky enough to be able to forage locally for hops and I love to use them as an instant, no-fuss garland and wreath (see No-Base Wreath, page 259). Shape it straight away and let it dry in situ, as it becomes super delicate once dry. Use hairspray to help prevent shedding.

Angelica: For giant dried stems, angelica is a real showstopper. The thousands of seeds can be a pain as they will go everywhere, so shake them off before bringing into the house and you're left with beautiful skeletal stems.

Love-in-a-mist (*Nigella*): Use this for its pretty, papery, puff seed pods, especially *N. damascena* 'Albion Black Pod' with its lovely, deep plum coloring.

Most grasses: These are invaluable to add texture to mixed arrangements. My favorite is *Panicum* 'Frosted Explosion', which I use dried pretty much year-round..

Scabious (*Scabiosa stellata* 'Sternkugel'): An annual scabious with pale blue flowers on wiry stems that turn into the most beautiful spherical seed heads that look like they've been sculpted from parchment. Most other scabious seed heads are a simple egg shape and aren't quite as pretty. Height 28 in (70cm).

STYLING TIPS

❋ Dried material is immensely useful during winter to keep you going when your cutting garden is dormant. I keep a stash of dried material to raid for Christmas wreaths or to add to the still lifes I put together when I'm styling my home.

❋ Many dried flowers are lightweight enough to be taped to a wall as a mini floral installation. Use a strip of decorative masking tape to secure a stem to the wall. Try the stem upside down, as that can work, too.

❋ Mix dry material with fresh – there are no rules to say they need to be kept separate. The benefit is there's no need for dried plants to be in water, so you won't be restricted as to where you position them. I find dried grasses particularly useful for filling in gaps in displays – they can be nestled between the other flowers easily.

OPPOSITE: Sculptural stems of angelica in an urn alongside mixed ornamental onions and grasses, *Scabiosa stellata* 'Sternkugel' and gathered feathers.

Gifts

The joy of growing your own flowers is that you'll have an abundance of blooms and no doubt want to share them with others. One of my favorite things to do is to send a friend home with a bunch – or better still a bucket of blooms that they've had the pleasure of picking themselves. Recycle all your glass jars as they will become invaluable as impromptu vases when you're sending friends home with a small bunch.

STYLING TIPS

❋ Don't try to mimic how a florist would do things – celebrate that the flowers have come from your garden and that they've been grown and cared for by you, not bought from a store.

❋ A few mixed jam-jar arrangements make a lovely gift when they are packed into a crate or box. The recipient has the pleasure of positioning them about the house, without having to put together the arrangements. This is especially useful to take to a party or a dinner.

❋ For a hand-tied bouquet, I don't bother with the usual cellophane and instead keep things as simple as possible and use newspaper. When I'm sending friends home with flowers, the paper is there to protect the petals during transit. It can be secured with string if you like. See also the Hand-Tied Posy on page 243.

❋ For a special gift, I'll wrap the bunch in tissue paper or wrapping paper. I buy tissue paper as sheets in bulk online rather than folded and stock up at Christmas on rolls of wrapping paper (stripes/dots/plain navy, gray, and rose) as it's much easier to find tasteful papers at the right price at that time of year.

❋ Rather than making up one big bouquet, I'll sometimes gift a bucket of flowers so that the recipient can have the joy of arranging them in their own way. It's always very well received.

TOP: A tissue-paper wrapped late summer bouquet of tuberose, dusty miller 'New Look' and bishop's flower
ABOVE: A bucketful of dahlias.
OPPOSITE: Jam-jar arrangements of dahlias, roses mint, and bishop's flower in a vintage wooden crate.

Resources

AVON BULBS
www.avonbulbs.co.uk
A large selection of vase worthy top quality flowering bulbs.

CHILTERN SEEDS
www.chilternseeds.co.uk
Top quality seed in unusual and interesting cut flower seed varieties – perfect for the grower who wants something a little out of the ordinary.

CLAIRE AUSTIN
www.claireaustin-hardyplants.co.uk
Specialist nursery of hardy plants, including a fantastic collection of peonies.

CROCUS
www.crocus.co.uk
Online nursery with a large range of perennials, shrubs, climbers, and trees.

DAVID AUSTIN
www.davidaustin.com
Specialist rose grower and breeder of English Roses with excellent pre- and post-sales support. Based in the UK, but ships internationally.

FLORET
www.floretflowers.com
Flower farmer extraordinaire, Erin Benzakein's online shop has a fantastic range of seeds and bulbs with masses of useful growing advice. USA based, but ships seed to UK and EU.

GREENHOUSE SENSATION
www.greenhousesensation.co.uk
Online suppliers of general garden sundries including my beloved Vitopod propagator.

GREENHOUSE STORES
www.greenhousestores.co.uk
Online retailer of good-quality timber greenhouses at accessible prices. My greenhouse is their 'Swallow Raven' design painted in 'Midnight Blue'.

HIGGLEDY GARDEN
www.higgledygarden.com
Wonderfully descriptive text and online info from seed supplier, Benjamin Ranyard that never fails to cheer. A great place to start for beginners.

H W HYDE & SON
www.hwhyde.com
Specialist grower of lilies as well as other bulbs. Expert growing information online.

IMPLEMENTATIONS
www.implementations.co.uk
Stunning bronze gardening tools (made from copper with a little bit of tin) – almost too beautiful to use. The copper is thought to help deter slugs and snails.

JOHNNY'S SEEDS
www.johnnyseed.com
Fantastic collection of quality seed with really useful growing advice. USA based, but ships internationally.

KELWAYS
www.kelways.co.uk
Specialist growers of top-quality peonies founded in 1851.

LADBROOKE SOILBLOCKERS
www.soilblockers.co.uk
Manufacturers and retailers of easy-to-use quality handheld and standing soil blockers. Great supplies if you're wanting to reduce your plastic use in the garden.

NATIONAL DAHLIA COLLECTION
www.nationaldahliacollection.co.uk
A vast collection of dahlias, available as cuttings and tubers.

PETER NYSSEN
www.peternyssen.com
Online supplier of quality bulbs with new varieties each year.

ROGER PARSONS SWEET PEAS
www.rpsweetpeas.com
Holds the national collection of sweet peas and other Lathyrus species. A fantastic range of top-quality seeds with excellent (and cost effective) multi-pack collections.

SARAH RAVEN
www.sarahraven.com
A wide range of carefully curated top-quality seeds, bulbs, and plants – many tried and tested especially for cutting, plus floristry and gardening supplies. A wealth of knowledge online.

SEEDAHOLIC
www.seedaholic.com
Beautifully packaged seed that comes with detailed sowing and growing advice

BE INSPIRED

Instagram is a great place to share ideas and be inspired. Come and visit me @clarenolanuk For more floral inspiration, check out my favorite instagrammers:

@beckycrowley

@bluecarrot

@floretflower

@flowersfromthefarm

@gandgorgeousflowers

@misspickering

@paulstickland

@scarletandviolet

@thomasbloomflowers

@underthefloralspell

index

Page numbers in italic refer
to illustrations

Acknowledgements

Creating this book has been an enormous personal undertaking, a project close to my heart that has filled me with joy. It began life over five years ago as a small seed of an idea that gradually blossomed into this book.

Thank you, Kyle Cathie, for believing in me and my little sketchbook of ideas - it has been such a privilege to work with you – I am so grateful that our lives connected when they did. Thank you for keeping the faith as the years rolled by and giving me the confidence to take the photographs myself – you have made yet another dream come true for me.

The wonderful team at Kyle Books, both in-house and out, especially Sophie Allen, my editor, for keeping everything on track and designer Lucy Gowans for her beautiful layouts; Isabel Gonzalez-Prendergast, for the late nights at the office sorting through the ridiculous number of images that this book swallowed up.

Thank you to Sue Peart, my editor at YOU magazine for allowing me to take on this project alongside my role while at YOU and for always being 100 percent behind me.

There are many incredible teachers and friends who have been part of my floral journey always – so many florists and growers who have inspired me and I'll also be thankful for, but two in particular: Sarah Raven and Erin Benzakine of Floret Flower Farm – both so generous in sharing their amazing insight and knowledge. Thanks also to Graham Talbot, my RHS horticulture diploma teacher at night school – you helped me make sense of the science behind flowers. Paul Debois for helping me get a better handle on garden photography (and the dreaded Lightroom), you have such an incredible eye . . . I have so much more to learn.

Thank you to my father-in-law, Paul, and his wife, Fran, for being my cutting garden guardians during a much-needed family break in the height of growing season and making sure all my horticultural babies were safe and sound and remained photo worthy.

Working on this book has taken up a huge chunk of family life, in particular over the past year as the looming deadline grew ever closer. Thank you, Harriot, for keeping my babes happy and safe on the days I worked. A special thank you goes to my sister, Sharon, for always being there for me; my constant cheerleader, and for looking after my boys when the deadlines were in danger of spinning out of control. Also, my nieces Imogen, Georgina and Hannah for keeping Alexander and William entertained while I snapped away at the bottom of the garden.

Apologies go out to all my friends and family for disappearing off the radar and becoming even more of a recluse than usual; thanks for hanging in there.

And finally, a special thanks to my husband, Jonathan, for his unfailing support of all the plans I'm continually hatching and for his unfaltering belief that all will come good. Thank you also for turning a blind eye as our lawn gradually shrinks and is replaced by flower beds and meadow . . . and for putting in all those hours of watering in what turned out to be the hottest, driest summer in forty-odd years.